IMPLEMENTI
LEADE

Angle
Main

read a
return
Pls :)

IMPLEMENTING SERVANT LEADERSHIP

Stories from the Field

Don M. Frick

D.B. Reinhart Institute for Ethics in Leadership

VITERBO UNIVERSITY
LA CROSSE, WISCONSIN

ISBN 13: 978-0-9816896-2-3

D.B. Reinhart Institute for Ethics in Leadership
Viterbo University
900 Viterbo Drive
La Crosse, WI 54601
www.viterbo.edu/ethics

Design and composition by Robert Schreur
Printed by Publishers ExpressPress, Ladysmith, Wisconsin

The D.B. Reinhart Institute for Ethics in Leadership is located
on the campus of Viterbo University in La Crosse, Wisconsin.
Its mission is to promote the concept of ethics in leadership as
integral to the advancement of American society and to ad-
vance leadership and ethics through publications, courses, con-
ferences, workshops, and public forums.

To my colleagues and students in
Viterbo University's Master of Arts
in Servant Leadership program,
in appreciation for the astounding ways
in which they have taught and inspired me.

CONTENTS

THIS IS A BOOK OF STORIES about how servant leadership is being implemented in organizations. Dr. Kent Keith, author and Director of the Greenleaf Center for Servant Leadership in Indianapolis, says that one of the most common questions he gets is, "How do you integrate servant leadership into the ethos and operating policies of an organization?" The prevailing mental model for implementing any new agenda is:

1) A few people study the principles involved, do a cost-benefit analysis and other research,
2) settle on details of how the new operating practices will be implemented,
3) get approval of top management,
4) create communication vehicles to explain the change and disseminate them widely and, finally,
5) "get buy-in" (compliance) from employees.

That is a logical, top-down way of looking at change management, but not always the most soulful way. Servant leadership is a journey, not a project.

Even though Robert Greenleaf believed we all needed to learn as much as possible about the skills and competencies of servant-leaders, the vital process was about *seeking, discovery* and *reflection*. Individuals and organizations *seek* a better, more humane way of living in integrity, *discover* the servant-leader within themselves and its potential in their organizations, and then *reflect* together on how to widen the circle of servanthood so that it embraces persons and policies, missions and mandates. After doing the head and heart work and modeling servant leadership, implementation proceeds organically, backed by smart strategy and wide-ranging and inclusive communications.

Some of the people mentioned in this book are my living heroes—Bob Ferguson of TDIndustries; Ann McGee-Cooper of Ann McGee-Cooper and Associates; Pastor Jerome Pienaar and Marlon Fortuin of Cape Town, South Africa; Kathleen Fasbender of the Tomah, Wisconsin Veterans Administration hospital; Jenny King; and so many others. You have to seek them out because they don't write press releases touting themselves as servant-leaders, and that is as it should be.

This book was the idea of my friend Dr. Rick Kyte, Director of the D.B. Reinhart Institute for Ethics in Leadership at Viterbo University. His vision was that a person without any prior knowledge of servant leadership could read it and not only understand the basics of leading by serving first, but also see how people and organizations have implemented these principles in their lives and workplaces.

In **Chapter One** you will learn how the Veterans Administration hospital in Tomah, Wisconsin saw its ranking jump from near the bottom of all VA hospitals to the top ten after Training Director Kathleen Fasbender began an innovative servant leadership development program that welcomed applications from cooks, nurses, medical doctors, administrators and anyone else who was willing to commit to the demanding but transformative curriculum. The chapter is rich with specific source materials and principles for developing servant-leader competencies.

Chapter One also tells the story of how the Tomah Area School District implemented a leadership development program based on the successful VA model. Its early outcomes include both a dramatic drop in burnout rates and a rise in joyful, collaborative efforts.

Chapter Two profiles TDIndustries in Dallas, America's longest-running experiment in servant leadership. Robert Greenleaf himself was the consultant to help owner Jack Lowe Sr. transform the organization shortly after Greenleaf published his ground-breaking essay *The Servant as Leader* in 1970. TDIndustries Partners (their name for employees) and members of the famed servant leadership consulting team Ann McGee-Cooper and Associates detail how servant leadership principles are integrated into the organization's policies.

In **Chapter Three** takes you to Peaberry's Coffee Shop in La Crosse, Wisconsin, which was transformed into a true neighborhood community center when servant-leader Jenny King took charge. Profits went up, too.

Chapter Four introduces you to a group of remarkable people who implement the principles of servant leadership in their faith community located in Clarke's Estate, a poor settlement in Cape Town, South Africa, and offers reflections on the relationship between servant leadership and Christianity.

Chapter Five condenses the wisdom of many people and organizations who have implemented servant leadership in their lives and organizations and offers short guidelines about what works and, equally important, what does not work.

Chapter Six presents an "Executive Primer on Servant Leadership," based totally on the original writings of Robert Greenleaf. It is a starting place for readers who are unfamiliar with the concept of servant leadership.

My profound thanks to all who agreed to be interviewed for this book: Jerome and Charlene Pienaar, Marlon Fortuin, and all my other dear friends in Cape Town, South Africa; Kathleen and Robert Fasbender in Tomah, Wisconsin; Jennifer King of La Crosse; Bob Ferguson, Gary Looper, and Ann McGee-Cooper in Dallas; and Viterbo University's Tom Thibodeau. I am also deeply indebted to the many workshop and course participants through the years who risked being deeply vulnerable with a person they barely knew, simply because we shared a passion for servant leadership.

Rick Kyte and Tom Thibodeau, two of Viterbo University's master teachers and natural servant-leaders, were unfailingly supportive in developing and correcting the manuscript.

Finally, I am grateful to the learners in Viterbo's Master of Arts in Servant Leadership (MASL) program. They have been my teachers and co-learners.

Don M. Frick
Minneapolis, Minnesota
October 25, 2008

IMPLEMENTING SERVANT
LEADERSHIP

How a Servant Leadership Development Program Transformed a Hospital Culture and a Community

S ERVANT LEADERSHIP CAN BE CONTAGIOUS. Once it demonstrates its benefits in one setting, other organizations in the community will notice, and if they are led by people with the insight, courage, patience and commitment to make it work, a community-wide process of synergistic transformation can change everything. That is what is happening in Tomah, Wisconsin.

In 2002, the Tomah Veterans Administration Medical Center was struggling like so many other medical providers in America. A frenzy of government "rightsizing" had cut the ranks of employees at a time when the number of veterans served was soaring.[1] Then the Tomah VA's Education Coordinator, Kathleen Fasbender, worked with Viterbo University's Tom Thibodeau to design and teach an intensive leadership development program based on the principles of servant leadership. Before describing the curriculum, let's jump to the outcomes.

Before starting servant leadership development, Tomah VA's overall quality rankings were so far down on the list of VA's 122 hospitals that they were nearly off the radar—in the lower part of the bottom quadrant. In 2006, after five years of introducing the principles and practices of servant leadership to employees at every level of the organization, Tomah ranked number 4; in 2007, number 9. Meanwhile, in a separate, system-wide patient satisfaction survey that measures ten customer service standards, Tomah was the best in the country on one of them and had three ranked in the top ten. Leaders of the VA Employee Education System were so impressed they sent people to Wisconsin to investigate what in the world was going on out here and shot video of one of the classes. Later that year, Tomah's program was showcased as a quality facility program in a video shown to Senior VA Management at a conference in Washington D.C.

Kathleen takes pains to explain that a number of factors contributed to the dramatic change, like customer service training for all employees, but adds that, "there is no doubt that the leadership development program has had a big impact."

The astounding VA experience inspired the Tomah Area School District to offer its own leadership development program modeled after the VA's. The outcomes from that effort will be detailed later.

I asked Kathleen to share her wisdom. How did she and Tom Thibodeau do it? What can the rest of us learn from their experience? As she outlined details of the program, I realized they were based on at least three guiding principles: (1) Everyone can be a leader because everyone can serve. (2) Servant leadership is a journey—a *demanding* journey that requires individuals to not only learn and implement new concepts, but to take radical, personal responsibility for the situations around them. (3) We are all connected through the webs of shared systems in our work, family and community lives. A change in any of these areas quivers throughout the web.

Everyone Qualifies for Classes

Through the years, the VA system has offered its own leadership development programs, but most of them were designed for leaders with positional power. Kathleen says this was a "big mistake." She explains why an accountant may sit between a materials handler and a Nurse Manager or Nurse Executive in her classes:

> We allow everyone to apply for the program because everyone's a leader. This has eliminated the "better-than, less-than" feeling people have about the organization. Everyone's valuable. But to work on a team, you also have to know when to be a leader and when to be a follower. The Veteran's Health Administration is a very mission-driven organization. When team members are missing, you notice the void. It influences outcomes when someone is not there.
>
> There is another, even more pragmatic, reason why everyone is welcome: to harness the untapped potential of employees who are being asked to give, serve and heal more people with fewer resources—

and do it for the sake of service, not for recognition or money.

Curriculum Design

Designing the curriculum for a servant-leadership development program can be a daunting exercise. Servant leadership is, of course, a set of living principles, and principles are something that every training and development coordinator worth her salt knows how to teach, but those principles must be implemented by competencies. The problem is, most of us never learned competencies in school like deep listening, using persuasion rather than coercion and serving by being a good follower.

"You have to start someplace," says Kathleen. "If you think you're going to design a perfect, one-size-fits-all program, you'll never get started."

Kathleen started with herself. For months, she read, reflected, listened to the needs of her organization and had conversations with Tom Thibodeau and key stakeholders about possible topics and exercises. It was as much a journey of self discovery as curriculum-building. As a longtime employee, she was savvy to the ways of the VA, so she also paid attention to real-life applications and timely approvals by others in the organization. Kathleen offers advice on making a servant leadership development program relevant:

> You have to agree as an organization about the key things needed in your program. Keep redesigning those things to make them work as well as pos-

sible, and make them applicable to the everyday work that people do. If you give them many topics that have nothing to do with their work, you'll lose them. But if you can help them apply these topics to their work, it'll work for you.

The resulting fourteen four-hour sessions included books, ideas, application exercises, a project, a personal development plan and mentoring relationships—hard and soft topics, skills and servant-coaches, all blended into a powerful adult learning experience.

Joining this group is not a trivial commitment. First, consider the reading—five primary texts, fifteen books total, plus dozens of articles on subjects that range from burnout to storytelling. The list changes every year, but books on the most recent lists included: Phillips' *Lincoln on Leadership*, Greenleaf's essay *The Servant as Leader*, Jennings and Stahl-Wert's *The Serving Leader*, Blanchard and Hodges' *The Servant Leader*, Kouzes and Posner's *Encouraging the Heart*, Parker's *212°: The Extra Degree*, Cottrell, Adams and Baldwin's *Monday Morning Leadership*, and Rosamund and Benjamin Zander's *The Art of Possibility*. Participants receive copies of all the books, plus a few smaller ones released by publishers like Successories or Simple Truths, including titles like *The Leadership Secrets of Santa Claus*, Vince Lombardi's *What It Takes to be Number One* (a hit in Wisconsin!), *The Race*, *The Dash*, and *The Power of Attitude*.

I happened to be present at Session 13 when *The Art of Possibility* was on the agenda. Participants watched the video that accompanied the book, and then Tom and

Kathleen presented key learning concepts and exercises. Other topics that day included: (1) a recap of previous sessions, (2) Rejuvenation of Self, (3) Encouraging the Heart, (4) Humor, Storytelling and the Servant-Leader, (5) Preparation for Success, (6) homework assignments that included a leadership development-related success story, completion of personal mission statement and personal development plan, and a reminder to hand in a report on the personal project that small group participants created and implemented in the workplace or community, and (7) evaluation of the day's session. All that in four hours!

Other topics during the year may include Edward DeBono's "Six Thinking Hats," conflict management, the nature of hospitality, culture-building, customer service, mentoring, stages of personal power, team dynamics, change management, personality inventories and many others.

People and Processes

Kathleen, who I consider one of those natural servant-leaders Greenleaf wrote about, integrates people and processes. Processes are there to serve people, while people serve the processes that enhance the whole. She outlined some lessons learned about process and people after six years' experience of guiding servant-leadership development groups.

Do an Opening Retreat and Continue the Hospitality
Begin every new class with a retreat. Be hospitable, pamper people and provide food. Choose your environ-

ment carefully, both on and off-site, because it is the place to begin building community through common conversations, to begin dreaming about breathtaking possibilities.

Begin each class with a short, inspirational clip on leadership or a related topic such as those in the *Priorities for Life* series. Make the classroom a safe space by continuing the hospitality in every session.

Involve Coaches

Every class member has a personal coach, someone who has been through the program. There is a ratio of two coaches for every five-to-six participants. Coaches, in turn, are chosen and mentored by Kathleen. She carefully considers which coaches should be paired with each other and with participants, paying attention to their respective personality inventories, strengths, deficits, interests and work relationships. For example, a participant would not be paired with a coach who had a supervisory relationship with the participant.

Kathleen meets three times with coaches. They discuss what to do in coaching sessions, their expectations, barriers to learning, how to prevent participants from feeling overwhelmed and a host of other matters. She sometimes asks the coaches to coach her, too, and help with planning and presenting sessions.

Evaluate!

Kathleen Fasbender takes evaluation seriously. Very seriously. That's part of the VA culture. She asks participants to evaluate every class session and requests extensive mid-year and end-of-year evaluations, which inform continuous improvement. She considers evaluation an act of servant leadership, of listening and responding to real needs.

Become a Servant Taskmaster

Kathleen also takes seriously the role she calls "The Taskmaster," and considers it to be an act of servant leadership. She explains:

> Even though we have a core competency that talks about flexibility and adaptability—and I think we demonstrate that by changing our curriculum as we need to—someone also has to be a taskmaster to keep the program on track. It's very easy to get engaged in a topic that you had scheduled for an hour, and then the group moves it into the next hour, and the next hour. Pretty soon, you're halfway through the program and you might be 10% through the curriculum. So, part of my job is to keep us on-task when necessary.
>
> People sometimes appreciate that and sometimes they don't. But you have to do it, because if you want a level playing field for your employees and allow one group to get the entire curriculum and the next group to only get half of it, there's a gap. We're trying to eliminate the gaps so even our alumni are up-to-speed on the latest. The intent of the curriculum is not to discuss A-through-Z on every topic; the intent is to provide valuable and usable information with resources for the participant and/or coaching groups to seek additional explorations if interested.

Nurture Your Alumni

Alumni are kept in the leadership loop. They receive overviews and sometimes copies of any new books integrated into the curriculum since their classes ended, and are encouraged to attend four alumni sessions offered throughout the year. "Just because they've finished class," says Kathleen, "it doesn't mean they no longer need to stretch and grow as leaders. So we continue to try to give them the tools they can use successfully, because servant leadership really is a journey."

Collaborate

Kathleen was lucky to have the services of Tom Thibodeau as her partner-designer and presenter. Around Viterbo University, Tom is known as a master teacher. He can take a leadership book or an overview of Kantian ethics and boil it down to a single page. In spite of its brevity, the content is never trivialized, and is always, always, supported with stories, then resolved with application exercises. It's a funny thing about Tom and his stories. If you cannot remember the principle he talked about, you can always remember the stories, and then they take you right back to the principle.

Kathleen asks others to serve as guest speakers. The mix is different every year, but she and Tom are the anchors.

The universe does not provide a Tom Thibodeau—or a Kathleen Fasbender—for every servant leadership development program, but it does provide a wealth of information on how adults learn, and any of us can follow the principles employed by these two masters. I spoke with two teacher friends and asked them to summarize the most important principles in teaching adults. They both hold doctorates in adult education, but more importantly, consistently receive rave reviews from their adult students. As it turns out, their list could have been generated by watching Tom and Kathleen in action:

- Organize the content. Make it clear and practical.
- Involve all the senses.
- Don't be afraid of humor
- Illustrate and embed content with stories.
- Ask learners to tell their stories, too. Honor and build upon their experiences. They've had plenty of them, enough that many class members could likely teach parts of the class themselves.
- Encourage individual reflection.
- Give learners some choices.
- Build community; celebrate together.
- Model what you teach.

Share and Celebrate

Kathleen's favorite class every year is the final one when each participant is asked to share success stories of how the servant-leadership learning has affected their work and lives. "Some of those success stories knock your socks off," she says. Then her eyes light up as she continues:

What is learned here has saved marriages, improved relationships with children, relationships between grandparents and grandkids, and with co-workers. It has changed how they feel about themselves.

We had a fellow who was a fairly negative supervisor, but he was effective, got his job done and was able to move things forward. He never wanted to take the leadership development program, but a year before he retired, he finally decided to enroll. He said, "I should have done this years ago. I never realized how much growing I still needed to do and how I needed to reframe how I view the world." He said it was one of the best things he'd ever done. His relationship with the grandkids he was helping to raise changed dramatically, and caring for them became a joy instead of a hardship, something he looked forward to every day.

These are the things people are telling us about the difference leadership development is making in their lives. When you hear those stories, you think, "We'd be foolish to discontinue it."

The class participants I spoke with felt the same way. Leah Finch was new in her job as a compliance officer when she began the course. She is a young woman in a responsible position, and told me, "When you're young, you need confidence. This course has helped my professional development. I feel more confident, more willing to give my input. Every time I come to this class I feel revived and ready to go back to work."

Todd Weibel, Physical Therapist, was also relatively new to the Tomah VA when he enrolled. Near the end of the course, he shared his thoughts:

It's helped me come to the realization that everybody can be a leader. It isn't necessarily a title that says you're a leader. It's how you react to your co-workers and interact with them. I don't know that

I've gained that insight only from this class, but it's nice to hear, to be reaffirmed that that's a good way to look at leadership, that you don't have to be the one who everybody turns to, but you can be the one who has an idea to help, to maybe allow others to draw on that, and not necessarily be in the forefront.

Kathleen hears comments like these all the time. She has seen alumni promoted or hired away from the VA because of their emerging leadership competencies, and listened with deep gratitude as students shared their successes. "When we get to the last session at the end of the year and listen to each person's success story, that gives me such an overwhelming, powerful feeling of pride in what they have learned," she says, "not because of me, but because of what we provide each other. Despite the fact that running this program is an awful lot of work, if we can help make people the best they can be, then we've done our job."

Leveraging the Learning at the Tomah Area School District

In May 2004, Kathleen's husband Robert was hired as superintendent of the Tomah Area School District. He inherited what one administrator called a "culture of negativity, especially at the high school, in spite of its principal working to be more positive." Robert himself says the high school had outstanding staff and faculty but no teamwork or team-building efforts. Distrust was at an all-time high.

By the time Robert took the position, word had filtered through the community about the success of Kathleen's leadership development program at the VA. In the next three years, Tomah residents heard even more good news about the soaring quality rankings at the VA, and heard neighbors tell how they had been transformed by the program. At first, Robert was reluctant to push a similar program for the District because of his wife's starring role, but others urged him to move ahead because something had to be done for the District's morale and, besides, the expert in such matters lived in their home town, even if she was his wife.

In July 2007, the Tomah Area School District Board of Education heard a proposal to start a leadership development program modeled after the one at the VA and unanimously accepted it in one meeting. The cost: $65,000 including one-time start-up costs, not a trivial expense for a small-town school district.

In the fall, they all came together. Custodians, coaches and cooks, teachers, administrators and aides—all sat in the same room for the first of thirteen sessions. Seventh-grade teacher Mary Shattuck was one of them, and her story is universal for many teachers and non-teachers who are in a mid-career slump:

> I didn't know what to expect. I came into this not loving my job anymore and not knowing what to do about it. I was at the point where my attitude was, "I'm your teacher. Listen to me! Follow me! Do what I want you to do!" and I wasn't looking out there at who was in the classroom, understanding

what they were going through and using that to learn how to lead.

I always thought I was a servant-leader kind of person, but I just got bogged down by the negativity and by taking myself so seriously—the downward spiral. Not as many people have respect for education these days as when I started, and you get burned out with it.

In fact, I sat down with my principal this summer and said, "I don't know what to do anymore. I'm not happy. I don't think you're listening to me. I don't think I'm listening to you. The whole scheme of things is not working together well." Later, [my principal] Cindy was the one who recommended I do this development class.

Right from the beginning, this program was so positive. You're coming together with all these people who have the same goals you have. It's wonderful, because I wouldn't have known half of these people if it wasn't for this program. We're from different schools, with different types of jobs.

This training opened a whole new way of thinking and started me in the process of loving my job again.

Mary's classmate Greg Gaarder is Business Manager for the District and believes all administrators should take the program. He expected to learn about a "more project-oriented change agenda" that would address systemic change in the District, and was mildly surprised to discover was that the servant-leadership change agenda started with individuals, not systems. "Still," he said, "if student achievement scores increase and we have a better culture in our buildings, it'll be worth every nickel."

Robert Fasbender says it has already made a difference, especially at the high school, where an attitude survey showed that cooperation is increasing, and the divisions between administrators, faculty and staff are narrowing. Participants regularly appear before the school board to report on outcomes of the leadership development program, and in the spirit of Kathleen Fasbender and great teachers everywhere, offer findings from evaluations. Paul Weise, the District's Leadership Development Program Coordinator, had more requests to join the next course than could be honored. The class size is limited to twenty-five people and thirteen coaches.

It is expensive for the District to stage the leadership development course. Besides the costs of course development, the District pays salaries and benefits to participants and to the substitutes who cover classrooms while teachers are in class. To attend the sessions, teachers must invest precious time developing lesson plans for substitutes and are not relieved of any other duties in order to read the leadership materials and do other course-related work. Is it worth it?

The Tomah community is paying attention, and seems proud of the effort. One candidate for the school board listed her support for the District's leadership development program as a reason to vote for her in the February 2008 election. When a misinformed blogger attacked the District's leadership development program, he was promptly "informed" about its power and efficacy.

The District's curriculum is modeled after the VA program, with an emphasis on personal renewal, teambuilding, collaboration and some of the other issues that were most pressing for educators. The material is presented by Tom Thibodeau, Kathleen Fasbender and others. Like the VA program, the District reserves the last day of the course to hear participants' success stories. The session was scheduled to take about hour, but it took two-and-a-half hours, and not even the resident Taskmaster Kathleen wanted to end it.

People laughed and openly cried. There were tales of marriages saved and missions reclaimed. Many testified about how they loved their jobs again. One participant admitted to confronting personal demons during the course and announced plans to apologize to the people he'd wronged. One of the project groups put together a twenty-five-minute video for viewing on the opening day of the 2008–09 school year to show the rest of the District the impact of servant leadership development.

It was a great day.

Postlude

Just before she retired from the VA in August 2008, Kathleen Fasbender discovered she needed knee surgery. Friends and doctors urged her to take her last few weeks as a VA employee as sick time and have the operation immediately. But that was not—is not—Kathleen's way.

"I had to leave things organized for the next person who would take the job," she said. "But mostly, I needed to get next year's leadership development curriculum ready to go."

Just one more example of the "X-Factor" that makes servant leadership development effective: those who teach it must also live it. And although she would never say it about herself, others are happy to call Kathleen a congruent servant-leader.

FOUR DECADES
OF SERVANT LEADERSHIP AT
TDINDUSTRIES

D ALLAS-BASED TDINDUSTRIES is America's longest-running experiment in implementing servant leadership. The company has evolved from installing heating and air conditioning units to creating and installing systems for a building's entire lifecycle, including design, construction, operation, maintenance, upgrades and internal control systems. Recent major jobs include the new Dallas Cowboys Stadium in Arlington and the Cardinals Stadium in Phoenix, but TDIndustries' "Partners"—their name for employees—also have worked on hundreds of office buildings, schools, churches and hotels. Several years ago they spun off divisions to handle residential markets.

On its website, TDIndustries shares the secret behind the company's success: "TDIndustries strives to model the management style defined by Robert Greenleaf as 'Servant Leadership.' We firmly believe our shift to this culture during the 70s has made us one of the most unique companies in the country—it is to this practice that we attribute our many years of success."[1]

As of this writing, TDIndustries has been on *Fortune*'s list of "The 100 Best Companies to Work for in America" every year since the awards began, often in the top ten, and along with several other servant-led companies is in the list's Hall of Fame. Let's back up and see where this all started.

Shortly after he published *The Servant as Leader* essay in 1970, Robert Greenleaf noticed repeated orders from a man in Dallas named Jack Lowe. Bob called him up and said, "Hey, I'm interested. What are you doing with all those boxes of essays?" Jack told him that he'd picked up a copy at church and it made more sense to him than anything he'd ever read. These were the New Testament values he wanted to follow in his business. He was passing them out like popcorn to his employees and to people throughout Dallas who he knew from his extensive civic work. Even though Bob's relationship to church doctrine was different from Jack's, he was fascinated. Bob, Jack and their wives became fast friends. Bob and Esther Greenleaf traveled to Dallas a number of times to consult with Jack's company on servant leadership principles, and they always stayed at Jack and Harriet Lowe's home.

At the time Jack first spoke with Greenleaf, his company, then called Texas Distributors, was already successful. Founded in 1946, it took advantage of the tremendous building boom that swept across America after World War II. But they had several problems, including static profit margins and low morale. People listened to Jack's inspiring ideas about how people should treat each other and then went back to their old ways. Jack and other executives also noticed that when terrific workers were promoted to supervisory or management positions, they all-too-often flailed, and then failed, in their new jobs. What was going on here? Could servant leadership not only help the company improve morale, efficiency and productivity, but also spur the organization to live out the highest ideals that Jack Lowe wished for?

Jack and Harriet invited every employee to attend a series of all-day meetings at their home to talk about the state of the company. People went for the free meal and time off work, but quickly realized that Jack had not asked them there to sell a new program. He wanted to create a safe space for open-ended discussions where everyone could chime in on questions like, "What are our goals?" "What do we expect of our supervisors?" and "What do we expect of each other?"[2]

Greenleaf's essay *The Servant as Leader* was sent to everyone when they were invited to the meetings. The density of the writing surprised them.

> "Hey, Jack," his managers would say, "this old boy over here is a plumber with a ninth-grade education. You think he's gonna understand this stuff?"
>
> "Yes," Jack would reply.
>
> "He didn't really think everybody was going to understand it all the first time," said [Jack's secretary] Linda. "But he believed that they ought to be exposed to it. And [Jack] thought that he would teach them about it, both overtly and through example."[3]

The company's current Mission and Values statements are direct descendants of those earliest discussions, and you can find them on the TDIndustries website.[4] Other places on the site express the living principles of servant leadership in pithy, accessible ways:[5]

- Leaders see things through the eyes of their followers. They put themselves in others' shoes and help them make their dreams come true.
- Leaders do not say, "Get going." Instead they say, "Let's go!" and lead the way. They do not walk behind with a whip; they are out in front with a banner.
- Leaders use their heart as well as their head. After they have looked at the facts with their head, they let their heart take a look, too.
- Leaders are faced with many hard decisions, including balancing fairness to an individual with fairness to the group. This sometimes requires "weeding out" those in the group who, over a period of time, do not measure up to the group needs of dependability, productivity and safety.
- Leaders have a sense of humor. They are not stuffed shirts. They can laugh at themselves. They have a humble spirit.

Through the years, a servant leadership culture has evolved at TDIndustries. We will describe what that looks and feels like later in this chapter, but first it helps to understand their servant leadership development process.

Growing and Developing Servant Leaders

In 1976, Jack Lowe gave Dr. Ann McGee-Cooper a copy of Greenleaf's essay. Ann, who has since become an acclaimed author and consultant on implementing servant leadership practices worldwide, worked with TDIndustries to help teach their Partners about servant leadership principles and develop their capacities for acting as servants for people, profits and the larger community.[6] Every year, Ann and her team refine the curriculum based on feedback and current challenges. Gary Looper, a member of that team who has been deeply involved in the TDIndustries courses, offered the following outline as a snapshot of the three current servant leadership training and development courses.[7]

I. *Introduction to Servant Leadership*

All new TDIndustries Partners attend a day-long "Introduction to Servant Leadership" class. A half-hour or so before class begins, new Partners may notice an unassuming man greeting each class participant with a handshake and asking how the work is going. Many are later surprised to learn that this is the company's CEO Harold MacDowell. During his presentation he is genuinely humble, clear about his own sometimes-flawed journey with servant leadership, but equally clear about the importance of servant leadership values, and is always inspiring. Throughout the day, other Partners will speak to the group.

From the beginning in 1976 there has always been a class sponsor who helps teach the material, usually a supervisor or manager from the field who gives examples. Instead of presenting bullet-point principles, the sponsor tells stories of how he or she uses servant leadership in everyday work situations. Stories illustrate how, and why, servant leadership is essential to building the shared trust that keeps the company successful, especially in a tough business climate. The message is clear: we take these val-

ues seriously and are all in it together, whatever our rela-
tive roles.

In this course, Partners learn about the history of the
company, the leadership legacy of Jack Lowe and his
successor and son Jack Lowe Jr. They hear about Robert
Greenleaf, the basics of servant leadership and, yes, still
receive a copy of *The Servant as Leader*. The three major
topics of the day are: "Creating a Great Place to Work
Through Servant Leadership," "Leading through Trust,"
and "Collaborating on a Team." In keeping with the latest research on adult learning, this is not a day of lectures
and PowerPoints, but of a few "nuggets" of information
and lots of movement, reflection and integration exercises,
all resolved with real-life simulations and stories that give
Partners tools they can use immediately.

Within sixty days, Partners gather again for a two-
hour meeting where they review what they learned and
share their own stories of servant leadership in the field
and in their own lives.

According to Gary, most are not surprised at the content of the course. "These days," he said, "many people seek
work at TDIndustries because they've already heard about
the servant-led culture. They may not know much about it
yet, but they are certainly engaged during that first class."

II. *Servant Leadership for Supervisors*

When people are promoted to supervisory positions
and are required to manage for great results as well as lead
others by serving them, they sometimes feel they are in
over their heads. That was true back in the 1970s when
Jack Lowe Sr. figured that leadership development would

help keep new supervisors' heads above water, and it is still true today.

The day-long course titled "Servant Leadership for Supervisors" introduces Partners to some classic management ideas like "Theory X and Theory Y" and "The Pygmalion Effect," and offers new ones like an "Interdependence Model" that is as important in face-to-face management as it is becoming in online interactions. Partners learn how to coach difficult behaviors in a servant-leader way, and to conduct an "APPLE"—an Annual Partner Plan and Evaluation that requires both tact and directness. Simulations help them understand how to address what they call "Tex Borderline" situations. Issues such as getting to work on time, keeping a positive attitude and working safely are serious enough that they can jeopardize a person's job. If, for example, a Partner does not comply with a requirement to wear safety glasses, he or she will be warned and written up. If the Partner's behavior does not change pronto (as they say in Texas), he or she will be out of a job. No surprises.

"Communication is always a huge issue for managers," says Gary Looper, "and we spend a good deal of time on how to communicate as effective and accountable servant-leaders."

III. *Leadership Development for Long-Term Partners*

A Long-Term Partner's Leadership Development practicum helps old-timers keep the servant-leadership flame burning brightly. It includes a review of materials in both classes, updates on latest research and best practices, and dialogue on current challenges.

Ann McGee-Cooper and her team constantly feed information to Partners about new books, research and training activities, but the information flow is just as likely to go the other way. Through the years, leading Partners have kept up on the latest readings and writings by management and leadership authors and practitioners, hired authors and consultants to give educational forums and have shown a willingness to make theirs a learning organization. And because they understand that servant leadership is not a "soft, touchy-feely" topic, they like to validate their commitment to this philosophy with findings from management and leadership studies.

Measuring Success Through Trust

In 2002, then-CEO Jack Lowe Jr. announced that "It is not enough for all of us to say we believe in servant leadership if we don't practice it." He told Partners that if reports came in that someone was not consistently acting as a servant-leader, that person could expect discussions about their behavior. Jack was not on a witch hunt, but on a journey toward alignment between values and behaviors. This came on the heels of TDIndustries implementing an idea they learned from Synovus Financial Corp., another company that uses servant leadership as their deepest philosophical base—to measure success by two benchmarks: (1) business results and (2) acting as a servant-leader. TDIndustries decided to use both benchmarks for individual Partners, business units and the company as a whole.

But how do you measure whether someone is acting as a servant-leader? After long discussion, the Partners decided it all boiled down to one thing: trust. "I'm not bragging," said long-time Partner Bob Ferguson, "but we were ahead of Stephen Covey's son in his book about the 'Speed of Trust.'"[8] Bob then told me about three times when trust paid off for the company.[9]

The first was during the economic bust in the late 1980s when the company's bank went under and TDIndustries lost its bonding, a critical financial piece for an organization that builds things. To save the day, a majority of the vested Partners gave permission to use their retirement funds for self-bonding. It was a courageous decision, especially for retired Partners, because there was no guarantee they would not lose all their retirement funds. Trust literally rescued TDIndustries.

The second time trust delivered dividends was when the company decided to spin off residential services and trusted Partners to choose the best way to handle things instead of dictating a top-down decision. A group of Partners bought one of the spin-offs themselves and have made a tremendous success of the business.

The third time was recently when Partners, along with other members of a design and construction team, figured out how to leverage trust to save $100 million on a major bid and rescued the job for TDIndustries.

Character, integrity, trust—these related ideas consistently appear at the top of lists of what people want and value most in their leaders. Even Aristotle said that one's character (*ethos*) was the most powerful tool for persuasion. The Partners' next question: How do we measure trust? The answer was staring them in the face.

As it turns out, the people at *Fortune* decide who

makes it onto their "100 Best Places to Work" list by analyzing results from a number of validated surveys. One of them is the "Trust Index" that measures individual and organizational trust under five categories like credibility and fairness.[10] TDIndustries hired the same people who did the survey for the magazine to administer it to their more than 1,700 Partners. Then they tabulated the results, broke them down under their eleven business units, and created a giant chart that compared each unit's current Trust Index performance with previous years. Copies are made and plastered all over their offices in Austin, Dallas, Fort Worth, Houston, Phoenix and San Antonio.

Recall that TDIndustries measures success by business results and individual and corporate behavior as servant-leaders. Because of transparent financial reporting, Partners already know the numbers on their respective business units and have had conversations with their supervisors about their individual contributions to business results. Now, this externally-administered Trust Index benchmark gives them feedback on a key component of servant leadership behavior.

"The Trust Index is like the report you get from your doctor after a physical exam," says Bob Ferguson, "and trust is literally our lifeblood here at TDIndustries." But as we all know, the way in which a doctor reports results to the patient also has an impact on one's future health. TDIndustries has developed a brilliant way to handle the follow-up on Trust Index results. They use wise elders like Bob Ferguson to handle the job.

Bob was there in the 1970s when Jack Lowe Sr. held meetings in his living room and Robert Greenleaf consulted with employees in the boardroom. But Bob is not a mossback, either. (For non-Texans, that means he does not stand in one place long enough for moss to grow on him.) TDIndustries still calls on Bob, along with other semi-retired friends and colleagues like Ben Houston and Jack Lowe Jr., to handle important, strategic tasks, and nothing is more important than preserving the company's servant leadership legacy. Bob explained how these follow-up conversations about servant leadership work:

> After we get results from the Trust Index, I visit various facilities with the scorecard. I'll take eight or ten people from a business unit that's under-performing and invite discussions about why trust is down this year. Their business unit manager is not allowed in the room. That person gets a separate discussion. After I gather enough front-line information, I feed it back to the business unit manager, who is obliged to pass it along to his or her supervisor.
>
> People know that I'm officially retired, so I don't have any skin in the game. But they also know that I've been around awhile and care about servant leadership at TDIndustries.

Similar discussions happen with individuals who do not walk the talk of servant leadership, based not only on the Trust Index findings but on reports from clients and colleagues. Through the years, several have left the company because they are more comfortable with the old-fashioned command-and-control style.

Bob Ferguson does not believe the Trust Index is the only way to go. "There are a variety of survey instruments out there," he said. "I think the important thing is to find a good one and stick with it so you have consistency in your database."

Culture as Leadership Development

For more than twenty years, I have been privileged to visit TDIndustries' offices and meet people who have become some of my living servant-leader heroes. I have observed that their entire culture not only supports servant leadership development, but actively teaches and rewards it. A few scenes come to mind…

One day I sat in the lunchroom with three Partners, two of whom were dirty after a busy morning on a construction site. They were in the middle of a detailed discussion about Greenleaf's essay *The Servant as Leader,* and it was clear they had read it carefully. One of them told me he quit the company several years ago but missed his "TD family," missed the way things were done around there and returned within a year.

Later that week, I began a conversation with a woman who worked in the financial end of the business.

"How do you like your job?" I asked.

"I haven't been here long, but I love it," she said. "But to tell the truth, I didn't think I'd make it through the first week."

When I asked what happened the first week, she told this remarkable story:

> Well, part of my job is to get the court to grant a mechanics lien on the customers who have owed us money for a long time and can't or won't pay.

There is a legal time limit to get these liens. About my third day here, I realized that I'd just missed the deadline on a company that owed us nearly $60,000. Before I told my boss what happened, I packed up my things, because after losing that much money for the company, I knew I'd be out of a job in about an hour.

But when I told my boss, his response was, "Wow, I wonder what could be wrong with our system to allow that to happen? We need you to be our teacher and walk us through this thing so we can fix it." I was stunned. He blamed the system first? I'd been there three days, and I was going to be his teacher?

We found the problem and eventually fixed it. The existing software had no way to alert us to deadlines. Meanwhile, my boss called up the debtor and said, "You know, we were going to get a lien on you, but our software system was screwed up. Legally, you don't have to pay us a cent, but we know you want to do the right thing. Maybe we can work out something, no matter how long it takes."

The debtor was a good guy. He had been embarrassed to call us and was relieved to have a way out. Eventually, he not only paid back our money, but also made us more money through enthusiastic referrals.

Here is an example of policies that are not only congruent with the principles of servant leadership, but with Edward Deming's work. You will see this kind of thing everywhere, even in routine meetings.

Every meeting at TDIndustries follows the company's "Ten Ground Rules for Meetings," which are prominently displayed on the walls. They include items like, "No one dominates the discussion," "This is a safe zone," "Have fun!" Every meeting is concluded with a "plus-delta" evaluation. Partners first talk about the pluses of the meeting—what went well, what was accomplished. That is followed by feedback on the deltas—delta being the Greek letter that represents change. "If we were to do this again, what would we change? What, specifically, could we do better next time?" This has become such a habit that I saw one informal meeting of only three people end with a plus-delta evaluation.

TDIndustries sponsors occasional Friday Forums where Partners gather to hear talks from community leaders like the Superintendent of the Dallas School System, the CEO of Parkland Hospital, or presentations by authors like John Izzo and James Hunter. I attended one Friday Forum where a team of Partners performed an elaborate, three-act drama about understanding servant leadership, complete with a rap song. At another Forum, the co-founders of the Container Store visited and performed their own skit about using servant leadership at work. Sometimes, Partners just gather at these events to celebrate.

Quarterly Meetings feature financial reports from each business unit. Because this is an employee-owned company, Partners take a keen interest in the details, and they understand them too, because they have all learned how to read financial reports. These meetings are usually upbeat, but any leader of a unit who has bad news is expected to be humble and honest, admit mistakes and give an indication of what corrective measures are being taken. In truth, all business unit leaders are expected to behave that way, even if they bring good news to the table. The Quarterly Meetings usually include a ceremony announcing the latest recipient of "The Power of One" award, which recognizes individuals who made a difference through their individual servant leadership efforts.

Gary Looper, who has sat in on many meetings at TDIndustries, finds the whole atmosphere remarkable. "It's hard to quantify," he said. "One time, the head of HR for a Fortune 500 company came to visit TDIndustries and was blown away. Across the whole spectrum of Partners, she found humility, a willingness to learn and a spirit of hospitality."

I call this the TDIndustries Force Field. I was alerted to the Force Field a few years ago when a Partner who'd had a heart attack told me her doctor wrote a prescription for her to go back to work. He noticed that her blood work was always better after she spent time visiting her friends there during recuperation. I felt it when I noticed several house trailers parked behind the offices and was told that Partners decided more of them needed to learn Spanish to better serve their Hispanic customers and fellow Partners. My son Dan noticed it when he accompanied me on a week-long visit there during a break in his college studies. Since then, I have joked that they ruined the boy for a normal life. He keeps looking for a workplace that feels like TDIndustries and cannot find it.

The company is not perfect, as they will be the first to admit. But they also believe that servant leadership can help fill the gap between inevitable imperfections and ideal performance and behaviors.

Servant Leadership's Transformative Power

Tom Creed illustrates the transformative power of servant leadership. When I met him in 1996, Tom described himself as a "big, red-faced, round-bellied, ugly Texan." Then he told me a story about Jack Lowe Sr. that is also recounted in the book *A Partnership of the Spirit: The Story of Jack Lowe and TDIndustries.*

When Tom first started with the company, he thought Jack's talk about employee ownership, expanded benefits and caring for each other was a bunch of hooey. He just wanted to do his job, get his paycheck and go buy some beer, and he told Jack as much. Within a few weeks, Jack put him in charge of a study to determine whether the company should restrict the hiring of relatives. This began to convince him that Jack might care about his opinion. He was right. Jack was the kind of guy who admired a person who said his or her piece, even though Tom Creed sometimes drove him crazy with his disagreements and challenges.

That was the case during a day-long meeting when Tom nipped at Jack like a terrier, arguing and raising objections. Finally, five o'clock rolled around and the two of them stayed seated for a few minutes while everyone else got up to leave. Jack gathered his papers together, looked at Tom, and said,

> "Creed, you gave me a hard time today, every time I turned around."
>
> "Well, I didn't mean to give you a hard time," he said.

"Well, you did. You didn't make my side easy. It would have been easier without you."

"Well, I'm sorry if I didn't help you."

"Oh, you helped me," Jack replied. "You helped everyone in here."

They sat there a moment longer. Creed was wondering what had just been said and what was going to be said next, then Jack gathered his papers and stood up.

He came around the end of the table heading for the door, but when he got behind Tom's chair he leaned over, put his arm across Tom's heavy shoulders and pressed his face against his cheek.

"I love you, Creed," he said, and then he left.

Tom didn't move.

He thought. "Here I am a grown man, tearing up them bars on Greenville Avenue. What is happening here?

"You know, a guy that can say that to you, that can say those words, I didn't know what to think."[11]

Tom finally got up, went out to his pickup and cried like a baby on the drive home. Years later, tears welled up again as he remembered the experience that changed his life. "No man ever told me he loved me," he said. "I didn't think I was worthy of love from anyone."

The event changed Tom's life, and similar events have changed lives for decades at TDIndustries.

What We Can Learn from TDIndustries

- Educate employees, give them a forum to have their say, and take the time necessary to involve stakeholders in reflection about the servant leadership philosophy.

- Top positional leaders communicate their commitment to servant leadership not only by their own behaviors, but by being personally involved with leadership development efforts.
- Use the wisdom of elders.
- Provide servant-leadership development courses and follow them up with continuous learning, coaching and conversations.
- Provide fair procedures for accountability.
- Find a trusted assessment that measures important servant leadership behaviors and stick with it.
- Create a sustaining culture of servant leadership: implement congruent policies, tell stories, celebrate, be open to implementing new research and evolving training and development efforts.
- Measure individual, team and corporate success by business results and servant-leader behaviors. Find tools to assess both.

COMMUNITY, COFFEE AND
SERVANT LEADERSHIP
AT PEABERRY'S

> I honor the relationships I have with others. I think rela-
> tionships, partnerships and communities are fragile sys-
> tems that depend on careful and mindful attention…It
> takes honesty, vulnerability, integrity and creativity.[1]
>   JENNIFER KING

IN THE INTRODUCTION TO HIS BOOK *It's Not About the Coffee*, Starbucks executive Howard Behar explains what coffee houses—and all businesses for that matter—are really about: "It's about the people—all the people… If you grow people, the people grow the business. That's it…If you think of your customers as people, you'll make a connection with them, and they'll come back over and over again to enjoy the coffee and the experience."[2]

Jennifer (Jenny) King does not need to read that ad-vice in a book. She already lives it with staff and custom-ers, and embeds it in the policies of Peaberry's, the coffee shop she manages in La Crosse, Wisconsin.

Peaberry's opened as an upscale enterprise with a stark, modernistic décor and an adequate but limited menu. With all the best intentions, the investors and early managers followed the traditional rules about maximizing profits in the competitive food industry. "In the restaurant business," says Jenny, "it is all about turnover of tables. Peaberry's was not really a restaurant, but was still more than a coffee shop. Managers thought that the more efficient we were at getting people in and out, the more money we would make. For example, by charging for wireless access, they figured customers wouldn't stay long."

Jenny had other ideas, not only about how to make more money but about coffee shops in general, and she gave me a quick history lesson. "Coffee shops took off in the seventeenth century and were originally places where people went to discuss ideas, politics, current events and the latest gossip. They were community gathering spaces, and that's what I had in mind when I took over here."

Sure enough, coffee houses have always been places for exchanging ideas, and were even nicknamed "Penny Universities" because, for half the cost of a cup of coffee, you could learn from some of the greatest thinkers of the time.[3] Mozart and Beethoven not only talked music at the Frauenhuber, their favorite coffee house in Vienna, but gave a series of concerts there.[4] Voltaire, Rousseau and Diderot made the Café Le Procope in the French Quarter of Paris a major locus of the French Enlightenment, and not many years later Benjamin Franklin tipped his share of coffee mugs there.[5] Edward Lloyd's Coffee House in London became a favorite meeting place for ship owners and underwriters to do business, birthing Lloyd's of London.[6] And in my lifetime, coffee houses in Greenwich Village and San Francisco became favorite haunts of the Beat Generation and sixties folk singers. But mostly, according to Jenny, people like modern, local coffeehouses because, like the theme song of "Cheers" says, they just want to go where someone knows their name.

"Starbucks was originally like that," says Jenny. But sadly, she believes the famed Seattle firm has gone astray by not continuing to nurture community. "When Starbucks went corporate, they needed to move people in and out quickly. It became more like a production line and took the romance out of the experience. It used to be like a hand-made boat; now the Starbucks experience is like a mass-produced boat you can buy anywhere."

I had a chance to speak briefly with Howard Behar at the 2008 International Conference on Servant Leadership in Indianapolis. Earlier that week, the financial press had reported on Starbucks' dwindling profits and their decision to close some shops in the U.S. and cancel plans for opening several new ones. I asked him what was up. "Part of this is cyclical," he said. "But it is also due to the product mix, and maybe we've lost touch with some of the factors that got us here."

So, how did Jenny King get so smart in her thirty-five years? At Viterbo University she majored in Religious Studies, not business, and went on to earn a Master of Arts in Servant Leadership (MASL) degree from Viterbo. Through the years, she worked in various capacities at a warehouse, a coffee shop, several grocery chains, a convent where she cooked for nuns and as the deli cook in a co-op, where she helped start a union and negotiate the first employee contract. She also volunteered at the Place of Grace, a La Crosse center for poor and homeless people, and in other ministries. Eventually, carpal tunnel surgery interfered with her ability to do industrial-scale cooking, so Jenny began looking for a job that did not require so much physical labor.

Just before taking the job of managing Peaberry's, one of Jenny's essays was published in *Becoming Authentic,* the book quoted at the beginning of this chapter. In retrospect, one can read it and see that she was yearning to find a place where she could congruently practice her servant leadership skills and nurture others. "I am called to reclaim my authentic self," she wrote, "and live the life I was created to live."[7]

At Peaberry's, Jenny is succeeding on all counts. She has created a community—she and her staff actually call it a family—that welcomes everyone from students to older women's knitting circles to meetings of a drag queen troupe. Her employees are literally becoming "healthier, wiser, freer and more autonomous," to quote Greenleaf's best test for a servant-leader explained in Chapter Six. Things are looking up financially, too. The place was hanging on by a thread when Jenny entered the picture. After the first year, she reported a dramatically higher customer count and a 40% increase in sales from the previous year. Profits were also up, in spite of servicing start-up debts, adding menu items and staff. There was now a buzz about Peaberry's in La Crosse. People were coming early in the evening to get seats, especially students. Remarkably, even though the population of La Crosse is only 50,000, it is home to three terrific universities, and the student and faculty crowd can make or break a coffee shop.

Jennifer King is an articulate lady, so we will allow her to explain in her own words how she implemented servant leadership principles to generate such impressive outcomes, and we will also include a few comments from employees—Renee Cannistra, Ashley Lau and Jennifer Cernak, all of whom worked at Peaberry's before Jenny became the manager. The conversation with Jenny was frequently and pleasantly interrupted by customers, staff, suppliers or people who just wandered in and wanted to say hello to her.

Making the First Moves

Jenny

When I interviewed for this job, I noticed there was not a lot of life here. It was quiet, clean, and beautiful, with many nice objects, but it was all stone and plaster walls. Even worse, there was not a lot of word of mouth about the place. I asked people in the community about their experiences at Peaberry's and their impressions were not good. They said the food wasn't great—which was understandable because there were not enough people working—and it felt empty and cold and sterile. I actually saw the existing environment as a bonus, because it meant there was a lot of room for growth. The investors agreed that we needed to build more momentum in the community before profits could go up.

Renee

I remember when Jenny first interviewed for this job as manager. She was the one who, during all the interviews, talked to us. She'd smile and get more than just a cup of coffee, and she tipped us. The fact that she cared about us as employees even before she was going to be our manager really meant a lot to me. It has continued to be that way the whole time she's been here. She's always been very conscious of us as people. It's wonderful.

Jenny

I wanted to make the space feel more like a community. When customers walked in the door they would feel welcomed without being welcomed verbally. Many businesses "welcome" customers, but people can tell when it's a memorized mantra; neither the business nor the greeter means it. Good customer service is about taking care of people, helping them have that warm feeling like a guest when they come see us.

Understanding an Energy-based Buy

I think I have business sense, but I don't have the technical education behind it. Some know all the rules but can't run a business. But here's what I believe:

We are entering a right-brain age where some of the rules don't make sense anymore, even with the stock market. For example, there are a lot of people buying and selling online and they buy Apple because they like Apple computers. The buy doesn't have anything to do with the numbers. It's the same in business. I wanted people to come in here and say, "I like this place. I'm going to buy stuff in here. I'm going to keep coming back because I feel welcome here." It doesn't have anything to do with me knowing my gross profit for the week. It's emotional. It's a community-based buy. It's an energy-based buy.

I knew that we would promote an energy-based buy if people said, "It feels so comfortable in here." "Feel" is energy. We have learned from quantum physics that a change anywhere affects the whole system, so you don't always have to do much to change the energy. In short order, we moved in some old, comfortable couches and created a homey atmosphere. People liked it. That alone helped change the energy. Then we started changing things with the staff. They felt more comfortable, and that also changed the energy. More people came, which the staff liked because there were more people to give attention to. Ultimately, money follows the energy.

Sharing the Vision

We had a staff party right away. There was no homemade soup on our menu and that was one thing I wanted to change, so I made a pot of homemade soup. I asked everyone to come after hours. We pulled the tables together and had soup, bread, and wine. I said, "This is your chance to get to know me, but here is the vision I see for this place. We can go there together."

I told the staff that the two goals I was going to emphasize were creativity and hospitality. I wanted to give people the freedom to experiment with food or drinks, and I wanted our customers to feel welcomed like a valued guest.

I gave every employee a copy of *Becoming Authentic* and bookmarked the chapter where I wrote about servant leadership, my ideas about business, mentoring, and finding and living out of one's authentic self. I didn't give them the book to brag, but to help them understand the business perspective I was coming from. I know I would like to know what my boss believed in.

For awhile not a lot was said because they really thought Peaberry's was going to close anyway; the place wasn't doing well. I realized they would be watching closely to see if I lived up to my word by behaving according to servant-leadership standards.

I knew what I could offer, but during that staff meeting I didn't try to offer false hope. I didn't present myself as being able to do everything or know everything. On the other hand, I knew I couldn't just come in and say, "I don't know what I'm doing even though I'm making more money than you, so let's do this together." Instead, I said, "I'm new here. I still have a lot to learn from all of you. You have permission to suggest better ways to do things."

That first staff meeting was good. I wanted it to be relaxed, and to begin the process of building community among the staff. Before that day, some of the day people had never met some of the night people.

Knowing Yourself

I was the complete opposite of the previous manager. I'm not very regimented; I don't have a lot of rules and am not well-organized by conventional definitions. Instead, I'm an ideas person, someone Robert Greenleaf would call a "conceptualizer." I like to think out loud about possibilities, but because I come up with ideas and say them out loud doesn't mean we're going to do all of them!

The investors in this place are also that way. They'll come up with a dozen ideas: "Why don't we do this and this?" and then I need to play the opposite, analytical role and point out why something will or won't work, or why we should take a longer look at it.

Some on staff hear all my ideas and get nervous. They think, "How are we going to do all this? There's not enough time in the day!" What I had to say to them was, first, "Just because it's an idea doesn't mean we're going to do it. This is how I think out loud," and second, "You also need to tell me your thoughts out loud."

The more perfectionist people weren't ecstatic about my style. They often don't trust others to do something, and because of my German-Irish background, I understand that. I can also get caught in the perfectionist trap. For me, that translates into procrastination, because if I can't do it perfectly, I just don't do it.

Jennifer

Jenny's funny. When she gets into her perfectionism, I'll say to her, "Just think about that for awhile." She understands and laughs.

Jenny

I learned that I was working more than I needed to. It wasn't physical labor like my previous jobs, so deep down I didn't believe I was worth what I was getting paid. Even as a college graduate with a Masters degree, the idea of being paid for ideas seemed silly to me. If it wasn't something that took a lot of effort and time, I wasn't pulling my weight around here. My feeling was, if I was not making drinks or washing dishes or cleaning toilets, I couldn't expect my staff to do it. But what I discovered was they wanted to be able to do some of that to take pressure off me.

I wasn't getting my deposits in because I had so much to do—or so I thought. I wasn't getting the schedule done quickly because I'd cater to what everyone else wanted. I was trying to work in all these student schedules and all the time off they needed. So several of the senior staff came to me and said, "You need to stop saying yes to everybody. We'd love to do the schedule for you. You need to start telling us what you need done and we'll help you." At first, I wondered, "Then what do I even need to be here for?" but then I realized it gave them that extra responsibility that they wanted. They're great people, and instead of doing physical labor all the time, maybe they needed a challenge here, too.

45

Ashley

When Jenny first came, she was here 12 hours a day, 7 days a week, and was running ragged. She wanted to do everything. Finally, the staff went to her and said, "You need to step back and let us help you. You need to ask for our help." Since then, she's really improved.

Jenny

Well, what I had to learn was, if can't do it, someone else can do it. They may not do it perfectly by my standards, but it will be done. I'm lucky I learned that lesson because later I hit a personal wall that pretty much took me out of commission for three or four weeks, and my staff was prepared to take over.

When I came on board here, the outgoing manager was going to "retrain" me to do things the right way. He's brilliant with numbers, did a fantastic job getting the place off the ground, and handled many details that are not my forte. I appreciated the training, but had to be myself, even with all of my faults.

Making Changes

At first, we didn't worry too much about profit margins, cost of goods, and sales volume, because we first had to let people know that they were welcome and our food was good. Since our baristas (coffee makers) also help make the food, I wanted our staff to have a personal investment in the quality of food, and feel free to suggest changes. Scones are a good example.

Before I came, the policy was to not make any more scones after they sold out. I asked why and was told that any unsold scones would be a day old the next day. Would day-old scones still sell, even if we discounted them? Yes, they would. "Well," I said, "let's keep making them during the day so every customer who wants a fresh scone can have one."

Then we discussed the quality of scones. If we only make plain scones every day, we can sell them cheaply, but they won't sell well and we don't make any money on them. It was in the best financial interest of the coffee shop to offer scones that were interesting and different—scones that sold—and for that we needed the creativity of the staff. So when an employee asked, "Is it OK if I put almonds in the blueberry scones, or is that something we can't do?" I said, "Well, it sounds good to me! Give it a shot!" That was a change.

The staff learned that we would not compromise on the quality of food. I understand the need to be fiscally responsible, but if I see food that is questionable, I'm not going to say, "Just boil it!" to save a penny. That is neither ethical nor safe. Many of my staff worked previously in places where they cut corners because they had been told to do it. My instruction to them was, "If any food makes you uncomfortable, toss it." They don't need to ask my permission.

Another thing that changed was the level of staffing. Before, only one person was on duty at any time. That person took orders, cooked and served the food, and rang up the sale. One person could not cook and serve a lot of food, so this situation was very stressful. But the biggest problem with lack of staff was safety. At that time, we had an all-female staff, and being here alone until 9:00 p.m. just wasn't safe. Now, we're fully staffed so no one is on duty alone.

I told the staff that the customer is not always right. Say there is a customer who bothers one of my employees or makes her feel uncomfortable. Sure, maybe she can pass that customer on to someone else who is not bothered. But I've also told them, "If someone is being aggressive and nasty to you and you feel threatened, call the police."

They couldn't believe I said that, but in my several service jobs, I've seen customers go off on a service person just because they could, and the situation can not only become inappropriate, but violent. You don't have to take that just because you work for $7.00 or $6.50 an hour.

Renee

Jenny has always said, "Call the police if I'm not here. They don't need to be here. I'd rather have you feel safe than have people in here who expect you to be nice after they've been rude and made you feel threatened." That's not something I've had at every place I've worked. Things like that really set her apart as a wonderful woman in general and a great lady to work for.

Jenny

We flipped the policy of encouraging people to leave quickly in order to increase turnover. We wanted them to stay, and to come back! So I thought we should offer wireless Internet access as a service, like ice water. It's a matter of hospitality. Besides, I pay the same for wireless whether ten or a hundred people are using it.

There was a paradox in all these changes. In order to make more money, we hired more staff, extended our hours, and paid for more and better food. I think that's different from what a lot of managers and business folks are told: "When times get tough, you cut labor, cut costs and streamline. While you're at it, maybe you should close your doors earlier in the day." I think that was happening when I came on board. I'm the first to admit that it's a challenge to not get into that fear-based management of cutting hours and costs, and it's even harder when profits are down. "If you don't have money, don't spend it," the saying goes, and sometimes your really do not have the money, or, if you do, you should not spend it. It all depends on the situation.

But it's working here, in spite of ramifications I didn't antici-pate. For example, our energy bill is up 30% from last year, not just because energy is more expensive but because we're open longer hours.

Ashley

I got along well with our previous manager. So when Jenny came in with all these changes, I first thought, "Oh you're chang-ing everything. Oh my gosh!" It took awhile, but when I saw the direction things were going, I was on board.

Jenny

You need to be very clear about the changes you're going to make. I have found it best to bring everyone together and discuss the changes so we are all on the same page.

Making Decisions

I trust people to make decisions, but many employees here had not been trusted to make their own decisions, so they didn't trust themselves. Others would just prefer not to make some decisions, so I also need to honor that.

Renee

I think she tries to be conscious of whether or not people want to make decisions. She doesn't force it. I love making decisions about food products and ordering, but I'm not at all interested in the website. Another employee here is interested in that. He works with her on the website as an equal, even though he is still her employee. Ashley and I have been doing the scheduling since May. We asked her if we could, and she gave us the job. If there is a problem, she talks to us about it. But we are allowed to have that control and to work in different areas, which I like.

Listening

Jenny

I don't talk much about listening; I just try to model it. I think everyone knows they can talk to me, that I want that to happen.

One day after spring break six of my staff came in and all of them had had some traumatic experience. The mother of one was diagnosed with cancer. Another had a friend who was murdered in Mexico. They felt they needed to come here and tell us because we're like a family away from home. We tried to comfort them.

Ashley

A few months ago I found out my mom had cancer. She's fine now, but the first thing I did was show up here. Jenny and two other people I was close to were working. I walked back to tell them right away. They all hugged me. "It'll be OK," they said. "If you need time off, let us know. We'll take any of your shifts this week." It was great. Usually you would dread calling your boss for time off, but my boss and co-workers were some of the first people I wanted to tell. I just knew they would all surround me and be there for me. It's such a wonderful place where everybody cares.

Jennifer

Jenny is a real person. She truly cares. You can go to her with any problem. I worked with her before and also knew she was smart, talented and experienced in the food business. She's also creative, but sometimes I have to slow her down.

Ashley

Ever since she came, Jenny has cared about all of us. She made a point of getting to know everyone's role and learning about us. And she is always approachable. If you aren't getting along with someone or have problems at school, you can tell her, and she will find a way to cover your shift or just listen. She isn't just a manager, but wants to know who you are and what else you are doing. That is great.

Building the Community

Jenny

When we started being a positive, welcoming place we attracted people who were attracted to that, and they gave that back to us. One customer comes in at least twice a day and buys a Sprite. He's paying $1.05 for a can of Sprite. He doesn't look like he can afford it, but we've learned his name, and he has tried to learn our names. I want him to feel as welcome here as Patricia, the woman in her late 80s who comes in, or the high school kid who comes in wearing slippers and pajama bottoms to study on school nights.

My vision of the Kingdom of Heaven has always included everybody. Who knows, perhaps we more "traditional" people are the real outcasts!

We have church groups meet here, fundraisers, the local drag queen troupe, computer users, a German culture discussion group, board gamers, a knitting group and students. We also get informal groups of older men and older ladies. Not that long ago, coffee houses weren't so welcoming to older people, but they are welcome here. There's enough food for them so it's like going to a restaurant.

To me, that diversity is awesome! Large groups may or may not buy much, but we just open it up and say, "Welcome!"

We are also part of the larger La Crosse community. At first we did everything because I wanted our name out there—we donated gift cards and mugs, gave objects and products for silent auctions. These days, we more carefully target the groups we want to help, like breast cancer and education. We look for places where we can make a significant difference.

When you're a part of something, it's easier to work hard towards its success. The staff wants this place to do well, and not just because they're making money off of me. They're looking at sales by the hour like they're watching a football score. When we started to surpass any goals we'd ever set before, a staff member called in and said, "How are we doing today? Did we break $1,000 in sales yet?" They're not getting kickbacks or a percentage. None of us really are. I'm not buying that kind of interest. It comes from them being excited about being part of the growth of this place.

You can tell our internal community is thriving when the crunch comes and everyone on staff pitches in, when they're here on their days off, when they arrive before their shift and hang out after their shift, when they spend all day here working and then come back and do their homework.

Empowering Staff

Honesty is a high value here. There's a lot of lying in customer service because people have learned to follow certain scripts. I want my people to be honest with me and with the customers.

I've told them that it's a lot easier to impress someone than to make up for disappointing them. If someone's order is messed up and they don't get it right away, I allow our baristas the latitude to make it right. But we go beyond that.

Instead of only giving good deals to people who are upset, we also give them to people who have been really decent customers. Baristas can give dollar-off coupons or free drinks to anyone, for any reason, which a lot of managers would say is crazy. Maybe a guy comes in every day and tips well. The baristas have never had the opportunity to give him a free drink because that wasn't an option before. I say, "Offer him a free drink. Say, 'This one is on me!'" What we're really saying is, "You're an awesome customer." The baristas love that, and I like giving them that power.

Those customers often comment, "You've made my day." When customers are nice to my employees, that also makes the employees' days go better here in the coffee shop.

This is all part of hospitality. Take the guy who comes in every day and orders the same coffee. Maybe he never even tips, but remembering what he usually gets and having it ready when he gets up to the counter is the kind of thing that not only makes for good customer service, but also makes us better hosts.

Decision Making for List and Non-List People

I go through the decision-making process with everybody. For example, I don't drink, so when a wine salesman comes in and has four wines to try, everybody who wants to can come out, have a sip, and tell me what they think. One person may say, "I don't like dry wines, but this one is good." To me that's a good thing, because I can say that to a customer. It's not enough that I say it sounds like a good wine, smells like a good wine, and the salesperson tells me it's a good wine. If three people on my staff say "Yeah, you should bring that in," here is what happens: (1) my staff buys it, (2) they can sell it to others because they've tried it, and (3) I know that three different people tried a wine and all agreed that it was good.

53

The same thing is true with certain foods. We all try all the foods.

Jennifer

Jenny listens to everyone's ideas and lets them help make decisions if they want to, but she is not coercive.

Ashley

I thought it was very respectful of her to ask us our opinion and seek our input, especially those of us who had been here for awhile.

Jenny

I'm good at making soup and love to do it, but I didn't have time to do it. An employee came in and said, "I've always wanted to learn to make soup," so I began to teach her. For the first couple of months there was a lot of hand holding: "Can I do it this way?" she asked. "Is it OK if I do this?" I told her to play with it, to trust herself. But then I realized that I have a certain talent for soup, so when I say "play with it," I have the knowledge and background to play, but that comment is not one that would make a novice feel comfortable. Beginners need a structure. I realized that I can't just give everybody free rein. I love that for myself, but for someone who needs more direction, that's a paralyzing situation.

Someone who is independent, creative and a self-starter will take advantage of the opportunity to explore. Which brings me to "list" and "non-list" people.

List people want to do a great job, but also want to know they are doing the right job. They may have struggles figuring out what needs to be done, and in what order. They are not lazy; they just need you to tell them the agenda so they can do it well.

Non-list people see possibilities and sometimes wonder why everyone else can't see them, too. For example, non-list people may look at the people on the shift before them and say, "They were lazy. They made cookies instead of doing this other important job. They must have been just standing around and goofing off." The non-list people see possibilities and like to make lists for others, but not necessarily for themselves.

Then the list people can get defensive; "What right do they have to say that? They're just being bossy."

Part of my job is to understand who needs lists and who doesn't, and to take the responsibility for being sure everyone has what he or she needs.

Firing

Reading James Autry's book *The Servant Leader* gave me a new perspective on firing.[8] In it, he talks about how firing someone can be the best thing you can do for that person and for the company. I had several employees who created so many issues there wasn't much I could do. I wanted to help them, to be patient with them, but not at the expense of everyone else.

One of my employees was a person who did a lot of complaining; she frequently called in sick and claimed she was too tired to work when she was here. She had been fired several times and expected to be fired again. The comment that pushed me over the top was, "My God. I need a vacation! I feel like I'm being worked to death!"

I had to do something, and knew I should start by calmly describing her objective behaviors and the responses they generated. So I said, "I think you need to hear what that sounded like from my perspective. When you constantly talk about physical pain or how tired you are, it's not that we don't feel bad for you,

55

but it makes your co-workers feel like they have to pick up the slack."

"I didn't mean it that way!"

"When you say things like that, it comes across that way."

"I never asked the others to pick up the slack."

"No, but if you heard a co-worker say 'My back's killing me today,' would you then say, 'Hey, take out the garbage, would you?' No, you'd take it out yourself because you know they're hurting…So this is what I see you doing. I want you to be happy, so if leaving is better for you, then you need to go do that. If you're not happy here, you need to figure out what you should do."

The first time we had this conversation, the employee was angry. She felt attacked. So she came back a few days later and said, "I felt like you were ganging up on me and that everybody else here hated me." I said, "It sounds like that was your experience at your other jobs. But here, I can tell you right now that if your attitude changes, people will respond to that." When she asked, "You mean, if I try harder, I'll be OK?" I said I didn't think it was a matter of trying; it was just an attitude adjustment.

She must have made that choice because her attitude went completely positive. She stayed and became a team player again. As we speak, she is going back to school and seems very happy about it. Not that what I said had everything to do with it, but for the first time, when she was confronted, the topic was not, "You're a loser and you need to go."

I think there are distinctive differences with women, especially in the confidence level, that can affect job performance and sometimes even lead to a firing. I worked with a woman who I'll call Wanda at a previous job who was fun and outgoing, great with customers and personable. But she wanted to work for another place here in town because her organization was very regimented. So I hired her. When she put in her notice at the last job, they fired her on the spot, which devastated her. They had the right to do that, but she never thought she'd be fired from something in her life, so when she came in she was extremely slow and methodical. She even walked slowly. We had trouble teaching her anything. It was painful to watch. I thought, "Oh my God, what have I done?" And I knew her personally! The staff said, "Are you kidding me? Look at how she works!"

A mutual friend asked my new employee how it was going. She said, "I don't know. I'm just nervous all the time." Come to find out, she was so afraid of being fired here that she moved as slowly as possible because she didn't want to forget something or do anything wrong. It was paralyzing her. So our mutual friend called and explained what was going on with her.

I decided to just tease Wanda. I went to her and said, "So, T___ says you're worried you're going to be fired!" She said, "What!?"

"Relax. You're not going to be fired."

"Are you sure?"

"Positive. If you were on-track to be fired, the first thing we'd do is sit down and talk. Then you'd have a chance to adjust. Then we'd talk again. Then there would be written warnings. Don't worry about it. I want you to have fun here. You fit in here; you're good here."

Just like that, it changed. Now everyone says, "I love working with her." What's funny is, she's now confronting the people who are now her friends, explaining how she felt about their comments when she first started. It's amazing how giving someone a little confidence or freedom leads to such an attitude change.

57

Being a Mentor

I think I can be a mentor. Some staff older than me probably look at me and think, "She's got great ideas, she's enthusiastic, and she can run this place." But most of the staff are younger than me. They have no idea how little money I make, but that's not the point. I hope they learn that you can be honest with people who work below you in an authority position. Not that they should emulate everything I do. You should see my desk. It's an organizational nightmare!

Sometimes people leave and say, "I can't afford to work here anymore, but this is the best place I've ever worked." I know they're not here for the long haul, but my hope is they can get a glimpse of what it feels like to work where people are cared for, where decisions are made not only based on what's going to make money, but also on what's going to be safe for people, good for people, a place where people take care of each other.

Advice for Implementing Servant Leadership

I have some advice for people who want to live servant leadership at work and implement its ideas throughout the organization.

First, do not get discouraged. Operating by servant leadership looks good in a book, but sometimes in the nitty-gritty day-to-day, you're not always going to get it right. And servant leadership is not always efficient or practical! Sometimes it takes a lot more work to do it this way. So if you cheat a little here or there, don't get too down on yourself.

Second, it's important to know when you just can't give anymore. When I see someone walk through the door and I think,

"Oh no, not another customer!" I know it's time for me to go home. I've hit my saturation point and need to stop.

Third, allowing yourself to be vulnerable to your staff is not a bad thing. I was probably at my most vulnerable with my staff—and with everyone—during some personal turmoil this last year. I hit a point where I was not reporting in, and many staff had reached a point where they were extremely frustrated with me. "What is going on?" they asked. "Are you coming back? Are you leaving for good?" It was a messy deal. Several times, they saw me in here crying and at wits end. Then they did something sweet; they all pitched in to buy me tickets for a concert up in the Twin Cities. They said, "You're around here all the time. You just need to get away and go have fun."

But I still hadn't learned the full lesson. Later, after I recovered, I sensed a tension when I came back from some traveling. In many situations with a hierarchical leadership, staff would say, "Why is this person our manager? She's not around much and doesn't do anything!" But here, my staff confronted me lovingly: "We're really happy for you. We know you went through this awful time, and are better, but we really need you here."

When I got my head back on straight I knew I needed to acknowledge that I'd been missing in action. I spoke to them one-on-one and told them that I realized I hadn't been available for the last two months. "I want you to know that I'm committed to being back," I said. "I appreciate all the work you did while I was gone. If you'd like to tell me anything about how you felt while I was gone, if you were frustrated or whatever, please do so."

And they did. I found that many of them felt guilty for being mad at me. They said things like, "We really like you and care about you, but you made us angry and frustrated. It seemed like you didn't care about us anymore. You got us going on this track and then you jumped!'' Several didn't want to get into it, and I told them, "I'm your friend. I am always going to be your friend, but I'm also your boss, and this would help me learn, too."

Fourth, take heart from the fact that once the servant leadership principles are in place, they will work for you during the hard times. If the past manager here had mostly disappeared for a month, my staff would not have known where to order supplies, who to call to fix a plumbing problem, or what to do with staff conflicts. But because I'd given them the opportunity to do those things and allowed them to help me, they could do it. They weren't thrilled about doing it all, but they could do it.

Fifth, take your reward from the standpoint of doing the right thing. I don't make a lot of money, but I wouldn't go to another job I hated for three times this much money. I've been there and know the desensitizing that happens. I've been here, where I don't need to censor my political views or my personal life. I can be very honest here. That means a lot to me, and so does the fact that my staff feels like we're family. They bring their other family members in to meet this family.

A conversation with Jenny King is a breath of fresh air. In her direct, disarming manner, she creates a safe space where she can claim what Greenleaf called one's "legitimate greatness" and also confess her personal foibles, and invite you to do the same if you wish. She listens with deep presence, uses persuasion as her preferred mode of power, holds herself and others accountable, practices intuition and foresight in her personal and business life, and puts the highest priority needs of others at the top of the agenda, all while living in the paradox of running a successful business. These competencies are key markers for servant-leaders.

Servant leadership sounds wonderful, but it is certainly not easy, as Jenny explained in *Becoming Authentic:*

> What I have learned is that servant leadership is not for the faint of heart. Sure, at first glance it may appear like a feel-good kind of leadership style. I have even found that some people hear "servant" and think "easy" or "push-over." But those of us who have dared to look beyond the friendly exterior have encountered a life-altering worldview and a style of living that stretches the boundaries of possibility. If you are seeking to be surprised by what you learn about the world and, more importantly, about yourself, then by all means join us in applying servant leadership to your life. More than a course of study or a leadership style, I believe servant leadership is a way of being in the world.[9]

THE CHRISTIAN FAITH
AND SERVANT LEADERSHIP:
THE CAPE TOWN CONNECTION

So let us learn how to serve
And in our lives enthrone Him,
Each other's needs to prefer,
For it is Christ we're serving.

FINAL VERSE OF THE HYMN *THE SERVANT KING*
BY GRAHAM KENDRICK

Servant Leadership and Christianity

THESE DAYS, CHRISTIAN CHURCHES of all stripes have embraced the phrase "servant leadership," and rightly so. The words draw on two of the ancient theological traditions of Christendom—Christ as Servant and Christ as King. Robert Greenleaf once confided to his good friend Bill Bottum that the image of Jesus washing the feet of the disciples was in his mind when he wrote the first draft of his essay *The Servant as Leader*. But he made Bill swear that he would not tell a soul, because Greenleaf did not want the idea to be perceived as only Christian.[1]

He believed it belonged to everyone and always had, even before he articulated a modern version of it.

To be sure, Greenleaf was not a traditional doctrinal Christian, but he happily claimed his Judeo-Christian roots in Methodism and Quakerism and was a far more subtle and informed theologian than he let on. His friendships included religious luminaries like Norman Vincent Peale, Harry Emerson Fosdick, author and Rabbi Abraham Heschel, theologians Joseph Fletcher and Gerald Heard, religious historian Rufus Jones, various priests and bishops, and especially Ed Oulette, a lifelong friend from Carleton College who was a pastor and Greenleaf's key informant on the latest trends in theology.

Some Christian churches have assumed that servant leadership is only a Christian notion; others have discounted several of what I would call the *hard parts* of his writings on servant leadership that are not necessarily part of doctrine—consensus decision-making, intuition, foresight, persuasion as a preferred mode of power, even listening with presence. Everyone needs to customize these ideas, and Greenleaf saw servant leadership as a broad canvas that others could and should creatively paint upon from their own traditions. He was respectful of religious doctrines and never believed that servant leadership should itself become a quasi-religious doctrine. But in his opinion, too many Christian leaders he met with during the 1970s and 1980s were more interested in managing than leading, more concerned with strategy than servanthood, more focused on money than on mentoring. On the other hand, lay people seemed to "get" servant leadership immediately, and orders of Catholic Sisters "got it" first and best because they were already living it.[2]

David S. Young, a pastor and author, is one who connects the dots between Greenleaf's principles, the Gospel and organizational life.[3] He teaches faith communities how to use servant leadership as a basis for church renewal and to take the time, prayer and reflection to do it well. Many other pastors and believers are doing similar work, but I had a chance to see servant leadership being implemented by people who never heard of the phrase. They were simply living out the Gospel as they understood it, and they were doing it in another hemisphere. From my worm's-eye view, as Greenleaf used to say, they illustrate the deepest connection between the Judeo-Christian roots of servant leadership and lives of faith.

The Cape Town Connection

In 2006 a business friend asked me to travel to Cape Town, South Africa to produce a video documentary on Community Restoration Ministries (CRM), a remarkable faith community located in the desperately poor settlement of Clarke's Estate. My friend was supporting CRM and had made several trips himself, but he was frustrated that he'd not been able to "capture the spirit of the people and the power of their faith" in his homemade videos.

"What do you want to do with the final product?" I asked. "Raise money?"

"No. Just see if you can document the hand of God at work."

Talk about a daunting assignment! How would I know where God was at work? And assuming I thought I saw such a thing, how could I capture it on the screen?

I needn't have worried. My new friends in Cape Town knew right where God was—everywhere: within them, above their heads, below their feet, but especially among them. They also intuitively knew and lived servant leadership, even though they had never read Robert Greenleaf, Stephen Covey, James Autry or Ken Blanchard.

I have now made three trips to South Africa, savoring every chance to learn the profound lessons available there, especially the ones that illustrate how Greenleaf's modern expression of ancient truths can inform and enrich the spiritual journey. To understand the lessons, it helps to first know something about the setting and the people of Clarke's Estate.

The Setting

The first thing you notice about Cape Town is its transcendent beauty. Flat-topped Table Mountain is visible from every part of the city and is part of a range that extends southward to the Cape of Good Hope. Cape Town's sparkling beaches and nearby wineries, resorts and game reserves make it one of the world's top tourist attractions. But if you lower your eyes from the mountain and raise them from the beaches, you will see neighborhoods poorer than almost any in America.

South Africa's social system is still defined by race, and natives do not tiptoe around the issue. During apartheid, whites were in control both politically and economically. After apartheid ended with the election of Nelson Mandela in 1994, Blacks gained political control but whites retained economic power. That left out the Asians, Indians and another group that seems to have never had any power—the mixed-race people who call themselves "Coloured." That term is not welcome in America, but I will use it here, not only because the mixed-race people in Cape Town use it, but also because it means something different there than here. In America, anyone with African blood is considered Black or African-American. In South Africa, "Blacks" are those who claim a specific tribal heritage—Malawi, Zulu, Yoruba and hundreds of others. The self-identified "Coloured" people differ from their Black African compatriots because of their mixed blood, and, like many African-Americans, they may not know their precise tribal ancestry.

Clarke's Estate is a Coloured settlement. It looks a little like the south side of Chicago, except far worse. Here, a visitor sees trash everywhere, buildings unpainted and unmaintained since the government built them fifty years ago, drug deals going down, people showing obvious signs of disease, older girls leading youngsters in made-up games because there is nothing else to do.

Down the road is a mostly-Black settlement called Malawi Camp where people come out of their homemade shacks once a week to eat the food and hear the music provided by Community Restoration Ministries. Malawi Camp has no electricity, sewage, fresh water or hope. At least Clarke's Estate has a sewage system, but it doesn't work when it rains.

On my most recent trip to Cape Town I asked five, life-long Cape Townians—all white people—if they knew where Clarke's Estate or Malawi Camp was located. None of them had heard of either place. When I explained that Malawi Camp was in plain view beside the main freeway to Cape Town International Airport, one man said, "I've driven that road many times but I just don't *see* those places, and I've never met anyone who lives in them."

By contrast, I was reminded of the word "Sawubona"— the traditional greeting in isiZulu, a language spoken by about a quarter of Black South Africans. Sawubona means "I *see* you." I also realized, with some shame, that my white friends in Cape Town reminded me of myself; I, too, have tended not to see the people and places in the most desperate parts of the large American cities where I have lived and visited.

One-third of the women in these settlements are HIV positive. A drug-resistant form of tuberculosis is on the rampage. Kids without shoes run nonchalantly on broken glass. Food is scarce. The unemployment rate is over sixty-percent, and those who have jobs can barely survive on them. People have come to expect no help from the government, which continues to prove its inventive capacity for corruption. School is not free; kids must buy uniforms. The white schools price their uniforms high enough to keep out most Blacks and Coloureds, even though the legal barriers to integrated schools are gone.

During feedings at Malawi Camp, you see scenes that are all-too-familiar on American television: very hungry African children with thin bodies and large eyes, young adults who look ancient. But one thing you experience in person that can never be communicated on television is the *smell*—of unwashed bodies, of hunger, resignation and hopelessness. Paradoxically, you experience something else that cannot be captured by television's electrons—a profound sense of community. I say this with the full realization that any impulse to romanticize the poverty in either Clarke's Estate or Malawi Camp—or anywhere else, for that matter—is misguided.

In 2003, a war raged in Clarke's Estate. In less than a year, nearly fifty young people were shot dead in an area about the size of six square blocks. Peace was restored when the people of Community Restoration Ministries staged a march to reclaim the streets for God and for peace. Pastor Jerome Pienaar was at the center of the swirl.

The People

A leader goes out ahead and shows the way.

ROBERT K. GREENLEAF

Virtually every Coloured and Black person in South Africa personally saw or experienced the splattering violence of apartheid. Most of them personally know someone who was murdered, tortured or perhaps even died of rat poison administered to some prisoners. Take Jerome Pienaar, the pastor and a core founder of Community Restoration Ministries. When Jerome was fifteen, an entire family who lived one floor above him was murdered by government agents of apartheid. A natural leader, Jerome eventually joined with friends to found a gang and named it after us—"The Young American Gigolos." It became one of the most feared gangs in Cape Town and survives to this day. In his younger days, Jerome had cocked guns pointed at his head many times, and pointed a few himself. Alcohol, drugs and chaos defined his life.

Then he had a religious conversion and eventually returned to his old haunts in Clarke's Estate to serve as pastor to the people who had once bought and sold drugs with him. Space does not permit the telling of chilling and inspiring details of Jerome's turnaround, but it is fair to say that grace and faith saved his life. Today, Jerome is a smart, strategic, servant-leader pastor and a powerful speaker.

To say that Pastor Jerome believes in the ministry of the laity is an understatement. One of the first Sundays I attended his church, I noticed that nine different people led the service, and he was not one of them. I later asked him about it. "This is not about me," he said. "I've seen it time and again that when a minister makes it about himself, the church falls apart." Although he sets goals and does ministry planning, Jerome eschews most *rigid* long-range plans because "the God we serve is far greater than our small plans." He has no obvious grandiosity in spite of his charisma, and has chosen to lead humbly and courageously. During the days I lived at Jerome's home, the leadership skills and physical courage I observed increasingly reminded me of Dr. Martin Luther King Jr.

> Accountability is the taproot of servant leadership.
> ANN MCGEE-COOPER

Jerome's wife Charlene grew up in Malawi Camp. She met him during his gang days, endured the worst of those times, and eventually wed him to complete a powerful servant-ministry team. Charlene is a tireless organizer, a hauntingly-beautiful singer and the hardest worker I ever met.

A striking woman of both steel and compassion, Charlene once saw a robbery in progress that everyone else was ignoring. Then she literally "went out ahead and showed the way," jumped out of a moving car, grabbed a thief by the scruff of his neck, and urged her neighbors to help hold the other three robbers and call the police. She personally knew all of the perpetrators, because she had fed them many times. The police, who were generally afraid to come into Clarke's Estate, finally arrived and stood around watching. She dragged her robber to the squad car, threw him in and said to the police, "What? I have to do your job too?" then leaned into the car and told the busted crooks, "When you get out of jail, come see me and I'll give you some work." And that's what happened. Now, several of the former prisoners help with regular feedings of children.

"Actually, I saved their butts," she told me. "If they had done that in a white neighborhood, they would have spent many years in prison. But I'm also a leader, a community builder, so I'm not going to let them do that to my people."

Mentoring with an Edge

Everybody has to learn out of his or her own experience.

Robert K. Greenleaf

Marlon Fortuin rolls around Clarke's Estate in a wheelchair. Some years ago a member of the Young American Gigolos shot him five times. As the shooter was preparing to finish him off with the last round, Llywellyn, one of Marlon's friends, shot at the attacker, drew return fire and ducked as the bullet whizzed by. Today, Marlon's spiritual mentor is Pastor Jerome, one of the founders of the gang that Marlon's shooter belonged to.

Funny, intense, relational, smart and thoughtful, Marlon has emerged as a CRM leader, specializing in youth activities. The kids feel comfortable telling him how tough their lives are because they know he'll understand, and he does. He listens with intense presence, but will not allow them to wallow in their troubles. Instead, he leads them in prayer, song, learning and their own spiritual journeys.

Marlon is writing up his story so other youth can learn from his experience. An excerpt shows how he commands the kids' attention with his message based on strength rather than preachiness:

> Sometimes we get in a situation that is really bad because we allow people to walk over us, do things to us, or for us, that we don't like, but we say nothing. That's being weak, and it's different from being meek. Being meek means you will address something or someone in a soft and godly manner. Being weak means being afraid to say anything at all.
>
> You are special to God, the Supreme One. Why should anyone less than Him treat you badly? There are polite ways of letting people know what you like and don't like. Use them. If others take offence, let them. You are wonderfully and fearfully made![4]

Like Robert Greenleaf, Marlon has his own ideas about how to pass along wisdom. "People are eagles," he says. "We get them ready and then shove them out of the nest. If they fall, we bring them back up, work with them, and push them out again until they fly."

Henny is a product of that kind of "stand on your own two feet" mentoring. He is twenty-one, a brilliant drummer, a showman with a smile that lights up the African continent, a kid you want to be around. When he was a freshman in high school, Henny was known as a top runner, the fastest in South Africa in his age group. In fact, he turned in times better than all but the best college athletes, but he could never officially prove it. Because he was Coloured, Henry was not allowed to compete in the national tournament with white and Black youth—and this was post-apartheid. Most observers believe that he could have eventually made it to the Olympics, considering what he accomplished so early with no formal training.

Henny shared with me some dark memories of violence from his past, as did many other youth and adults I met in Clarke's Estate, but thanks to the encouragement, mentoring and spiritual influence of Pastor Jerome and others at CRM, and a scholarship from my American friend, Henny is now studying music with two of the best-known musicians and record producers in the country. Today, you'll find him playing drums at CRM and other churches in poor communities along with gigs with national groups, or cooking mutton for feedings, joshing with kids who gather round him like moths to a light.

Modesty and Energy

It is better to lead from behind and to put others in front, especially when you celebrate victory when nice things occur. You take the front line when there is danger. Then people will appreciate your leadership.

NELSON MANDELA

Onalisa is a devastatingly-beautiful young lady—just out of her teens—who lives in Malawi Camp. It broke my heart to drop her off on an unlit dirt path by her house late one night after a day of fun and eating at a resort, courtesy of my American business friend who wanted to provide an experience of safe celebration for some of the adults and youth of Community Restoration Ministries. Onalisa is one of the quiet ones, a girl who emerges from her ramshackle home with no electricity or running water and shows up day after day to sing, cook and distribute food to people who are in worse condition than she is. I've never heard her say a bad word about anyone or complain about her situation. Like so many of her other modest friends involved in the ministry at Clarke's Estate, Onalisa simply serves in any way she can—with modesty, sincerity and near-anonymity. She, and others like her, jolt me into awareness about how much of American life is centered around entertainment, appearances and narcissism rather than calm and effective servanthood.

By contrast, Sister Salome is a robust bundle of energy. You can usually find her by following the sound of music and laughter. She loves singing with the women and girls while they cook unceasingly for CRM's many feedings. A kid who needs a place to stay for awhile can always crash at Sister Salome's modest home. A pastor who needs a volunteer to do the thankless work that keeps a church and a community together need not even ask; Sister Salome is already there. I came to believe she had a doppelganger because, I swear, I've seen her in two places at once. As a Coloured woman who grew up poor in the apartheid days, Sister Salome has experienced her own share of tragedies, not that she'll talk much about them. She's too busy.

Everything Begins with the Individual

The forces for good and evil in the world are propelled by
the thoughts, attitudes, and actions of individual beings.
What happens to our values, and therefore to the quality of
our civilization in the future, will be shaped by the concep-
tions of individuals that are born of inspiration.

ROBERT K. GREENLEAF

Robert Greenleaf would have liked Brendon Adams for
many reasons, but especially because of their shared love
of music. Greenleaf sang bass and also liked to sit outside
in the evenings in sight of his large organic garden and
play his recorder, like Pan serenading the garden faeries.
Brendon sings, directs choirs and writes music so good
I've never quite found the words to describe it. The first
time I heard one of his songs I thought it was a South African church classic; the catchy, soaring, syncopated tune
built to a climax that had us all standing. Two years passed
before I learned that Brendon had composed this music,
because he does not brag about such things.

Brendon admits that he hated white people early in
life. In 1980, at the age of eight, he and his friend Malcolm were playing on the sidewalk when a group of government agents suddenly appeared and started firing at
everyone in sight. Brendon and Malcolm ran for their
lives, but Malcolm could not outrun a bullet. He was shot
dead at Brendon's side.

Flash forward eighteen years. Brendon is one of the
early members of Community Restoration Ministries.

Since the tragedy of his youth, he has nurtured his passion for music, which he believes has the capacity to not only inspire, but also to redeem those who make it and hear it. He decides to personally do what he can with music to rescue kids, heal hurts, bring people together. He walks the trash-strewn streets of Clarke's Estate and nearby communities looking for talent, and finds it everywhere. He orchestrates a series of open air concerts they call Friday Night Live, where young people sing, read poetry and dance. "It was okay if it was 'ungodly' music at first," Brendon recalls, "because I knew that eventually God would change that." Out of this comes an eighty-voice choir, as well as a cadre of kids trained in other aspects of the music industry, like running sound equipment.

Today, fifteen to twenty of those kids are working professionally in the music business. Brendon no longer hates white people; he married one, and they live in Minneapolis with their two young children. In fact, Brendon is the person who first approached my business friend at church and told him about Clarke's Estate. Brendon continues to compose what he describes as "music for praise and reconciliation."

When I asked Brendon how he got away from his early bitterness, he said, "I don't know. It can only be God's grace." Along with his music, Brendon wants to create cross-cultural experiences for Americans and South Africans. He has eagerly embraced the ideas of servant leadership and believes they can speak across the divisions of faiths, tribes and skin colors back in the place he still calls home.

Living with Awe and Spirit

There are only two ways to live your life. One is as though nothing is a miracle. The other is as though everything is a miracle.

ALBERT EINSTEIN

This powerful sense of awe and wonder is, to me, the source of religious feeling at its greatest depth.

ROBERT K. GREENLEAF

Some years ago, Sister Anne grew weary of coming home from work and seeing scores of hungry people lying on the ground near her house. So she started feeding them, using every spare cent and accepting donations from anywhere. Two years later she spoke with her pastor and asked if the church would like to get involved. He thought not. She left the church and prayed about things. Then a miraculous series of circumstances brought her together with Pastor Jerome. She became one of the founders of Community Restoration Ministries and joined with like-minded spirits to continue and expand a feeding ministry.

Sister Anne is widely known as a prayer warrior. Astonishing things seem to happen around her, although she gives absolutely all credit to God, and almost always prays as part of a group of other Christians. A few stories:

An infant is pronounced dead by doctors, but Sister Anne continues praying in the waiting room. As the child is being wheeled into the morgue, he begins crying. Nurses and doctors are in tears when new x-rays show no trace of the heart damage that earlier tests had shown clearly, the same condition they thought had taken the infant's life.

Frederick, a bright young teenager who fled with his family to Cape Town to escape the terrors in their native Rwanda, sinks to the bottom of a swimming pool after being baptized in the shallow end a half-hour earlier. By the time they find him, he has been under the warm water for nearly fifteen minutes and has no pulse. The lifeguard and EMT give up; he's gone. But not for Sister Anne, Pastor Jerome and their small community of believers. They pray him back to life—or, to use their more precise term, intercede with God to save his life—and he wakes up. They assume Frederick has suffered brain damage after so many minutes without oxygen. No way. He is back home from the hospital the next day, chipper as ever. Frederick told me that when he first went under the water, he prayed that he not die, but as he was zooming into the blackness at high speed, he heard the prayers of his spiritual friends calling him back.

Christians, Hindus, Rastafarians, Muslims—people of all faiths or no faith—knock on Sister Anne's door at her modest home and ask for prayers for friends and relatives who are sick, injured or simply in need of support. Shortly after my last trip, a woman traveled 100 miles to ask Sister Anne to pray for her mother, whom the hospital had just sent home that day to die. Her mother was immobile, unresponsive, incontinent. By the time the lady returned home, her mother was already talking and moving around.

I suppose all of these events could be explained as coincidences, products of flawed cause-and-effect reasoning or non-scientific religious superstitions. We Westerners do tend to be reductionists. We look for logical explanations that fit our sophisticated world views, maybe so we can sleep at night, secure that our facile reasons can account for seemingly-miraculous events. Having grown up in and around the church, I, too, have seen my share of questionable "miracles," and I can be as suspicious as any other Westerner. But I have investigated and triangulated these stories—and many others—speaking to people who were there, including Frederick. They all hold up. One of the most amazing things is the response of these Christians after witnessing events of an epic, almost biblical nature. They shrug and say, "Well, that's what God does."

I happened to be a participant in one event that I will never forget. Jason (not his real name) is one of my American friends, a highly-educated Southern charmer you can't help but like. During my first trip to Cape Town, I got an email message from a mutual friend who wrote that Jason had gone on a drinking spree and within a few days had lost his job and marriage and was living in a homeless shelter. During the Sunday services at CRM, I asked the community to pray for Jason. They made me his proxy, gathered around me in a circle and began to pray. The air was buzzing. A palpable force field surrounded me. I have never experienced anything like it. This went on for ten minutes before I stumbled back to my seat.

Several days later I heard from our mutual friend, who told me that the strangest thing had happened to Jason. At 4:10 in the morning, which, accounting for the time zone difference, was precisely the time my Cape Town friends were praying for him, he awoke in his homeless shelter with a start and decided to go on what he called a "peace walk." It was the beginning of his turnaround.

With these people, there is a thin scrim between "ordinary," consensual reality and spiritual reality—in effect, no separation at all. For all their human faults, and they are quite willing to confess them, they move seamlessly between their daily lives and the realm of what Greenleaf called spirit and awe—what they call the Holy Spirit, or simply God.

Raising Up Servants

The first order of business [for an institution] is to build a group of people who, under the influence of the institution, grow taller and become healthier, stronger, more autonomous.

Robert K. Greenleaf

On the second day of my first trip to Cape Town, I went to the hospital with Jerome and Charlene to visit Jerome's cousin Brother Eddie. He was near death, and the day we saw him he was upset because his right arm was now paralyzed. No problem. Jerome and Charlene prayed, and soon he was waving his right hand in the air. Brother Eddie told me that the church's great task these days was not to preach doctrine or increase membership, but to "raise up servants."

That is an interesting phrase, because it assumes that servants are already among us, hidden in plain sight. The church should find and nurture them, challenge them, ground them in the faith, and *raise them up*. Or, as Robert

Greenleaf would say, address their highest priority needs, see if we can help them to be healthier, wiser, freer, more autonomous and *more likely themselves to become servants.*

During the early 1980s Greenleaf studied two churches that did just that. Westminster Presbyterian in Indianapolis was an inner city church that had declined from its former glory in proportion to the decline of its surrounding neighborhood during the 1960s and 70s. Under the guidance of its young minister Phil Tom, and through leadings gained by prayer and an intense study of neighborhood needs, the Westminster community decided that in addition to their doctrinal ministry, they should raise up servants to be trustees on community boards. Every member of the congregation—and every incoming member—was expected to seek a place to serve, to discover and claim a personal ministry that fit his or her passion and benefited the larger community.

At about the same time, Greenleaf also studied Patchwork Ministry down the road in Evansville. United Methodist pastor Phil Amerson and his wife Elaine founded the then-innovative ministry that offered programs ranging from neighborhood economic development efforts to after-school arts and music activities, job training and a health clinic. Joining the effort was not a trivial matter. Participants were asked to sign a covenant committing themselves to the support of ministries in the nearby inner city neighborhood. Decision-making was by consensus and leadership was shared. If you were not willing to act as servant, you need not apply.[5]

Neither Westminster Presbyterian nor Patchwork Ministry made it easy to "do church," but both communities nurtured, challenged and supported emerging servants to "be the church," to do the radical work of the Gospel—and of authentic servant leadership.[6]

Brother Eddie died not long after I met him, highly admired as a servant who was a warrior at *raising up* people. I only spoke with him once, but I miss him.

Community and Celebration

> The servant always accepts and empathizes, never rejects.
> The servant as leader always empathizes, always accepts
> the person but sometimes refuses to accept some of the
> person's effort or performance as good enough.
>
> ROBERT K. GREENLEAF

The last time I visited a CRM worship service, a woman was publicly welcomed back into the congregation after being released from prison. She had spent over a decade incarcerated for murdering her children because she did not want them to live the kind of life she had lived. Even though any thoughtful person would recoil from this horrific past, the church members still accepted her as one of them. They even had a little ceremony to acknowledge her return.

The CRM worship service is a place where anyone can demonstrate a skill to Christian brothers and sisters—dancing, judo, singing, drumming, you name it. Young people are especially encouraged to show their stuff, which need not be "religious" in nature. Yet, for these people, any growth edge seems to have a religious dimension.

> Community [is] the lost knowledge of these times.
>
> If it ain't fun, it won't get done!
>
> ROBERT K. GREENLEAF

This profound sense of community continues outside the church, and it reminds me of the fun and connectedness I experienced growing up in small towns during the 1950s. Let me describe a typical scene, one I experienced many times in Clarke's Estate.

It is the night before a concert and feeding, and the action is happening at the home of Pastor Jerome and Charlene, the social and spiritual center of Clarke's Estate. One large room of the Pienaars' exceedingly-modest home is devoted to food preparation. The women and girls mostly reign in this area, cutting vegetables, cooking stew, packaging food for the next day, telling funny stories and singing. And my, oh my, can they sing! Thrilling, chilling music of interweaved harmony and complex rhythm—everything from gospel songs to South African anthems.

Outside in the back yard, girls play silly games around a table and young boys squeal and chase each other while the men and older boys cook mutton on grills until the early morning hours. All manner of people from the neighborhood show up to help—long-time drug dealers, young men just out of prison, relatives, and relatives of relatives. The main form of entertainment is telling stories, and can they tell stories! Many tales use humor to redeem the scary events of apartheid days or gang confrontations. Other narratives are just flat-out funny, and sprinkled in between are comfortable conversations about people and events. Later in the evening a husband and wife show up who both hold Ph.D.s. They join in the cooking and storytelling. Later, a nationally-known songwriter and comedian who grew up in Clarke's Estate comes by and does several hilarious routines, including one that mimics Nelson Mandela.

Through all this, I am not an outsider observing community; I am immediately accepted as part of it. They tell jokes on me too, and listen to my stories. A federal bank examiner who accompanied us on a trip to Cape Town was so touched by the community he experienced in Clarke's Estate that he returned home dissatisfied with the somewhat forced, homogenous and isolated version of community offered by his large church. He is now searching for a new church that can provide something closer to what he experienced in Cape Town.

No Press Releases—Just Servanthood

A servant-leader is servant *first*… [and] is sharply different from the person who is *leader* first, perhaps because of the need to assuage an unusual power drive or to acquire material possessions.

Robert K. Greenleaf

So many people and images flood memories of Clarke's Estate: Connie and his warm, welcoming family who make feeding the poor a weekly ritual, even though he does not belong to any church; Freddie and Eugene, who took vacation time to help shoot video with me; the Muslim butcher who was embarrassed when I saw him slip extra mutton into a large order of meat Charlene bought for feeding the children at Malawi camp. "They're help-ing the kids, so I help them," he explained. Then there is "Jerome P.," a world-class keyboard player who has made CRM his spiritual home, even though his father pastors another church; the auto mechanic who donates repairs of vehicles used to carry food and concert equipment to neighborhoods where CRM conducts feedings. I think of Yvonne, Marlon's girlfriend and a brilliant young de-signer, and Marlon's sister Michelle, who laughed as she cut my hair in a living room because I was her first white customer. Nageve was my unofficial bodyguard, always nearby, always positive. Rowena, another quiet one, lost her father to AIDS, but touches people deeply when she speaks of her faith.

I remember the Muslim man who told me that he felt a tingling power when he prayed with the men of Com-munity Restoration Ministries. "There is only one God," he said, "One God!" Christians, Muslims, churched and un-churched, they all serve in whatever ways they can, and none of them has ever written a press release touting their efforts.

In two subsequent trips to Cape Town, my love for these people has grown. I have told my two sons, "Never go to Africa unless you are ready to lose your heart"—and, paradoxically, to watch it grow.

Q & A—Christianity and Servant Leadership

In the years since I first became involved with servant leadership in 1986, I have consistently heard three or four questions that betray confusion about the relationship between servant leadership (as formulated by Robert Green-leaf) and Christianity. Greenleaf, a Quaker, heard many of these same questions during his lifetime (1904–1990) and patiently tried to answer them.

Q: Does servant leadership position itself as an alternative creed to the Christian Gospel? Is it a kind of sect?

A: No, and Bob Greenleaf would come back from the grave to haunt anyone who suggested such a thing. He took extraordinary efforts to prevent his writings from be-ing interpreted as the basis for a sect of any faith tradition. Because servant leadership is based on a universal human impulse—the desire to serve—he hoped it could inform any and all faith traditions, every one of which already has something like servant leadership in its creeds.

Q: Can one be a servant-leader and not be a Christian?

A: Of course, but Greenleaf himself believed that the servant-leader journey was ultimately spiritual in nature, and he argued that a servant needed an inner, sustaining spirit (*entheos*) that may or may not emerge from a purely Christian orientation.[7]

Q: Can one be a Christian and not be a servant-leader?

A: That depends on how you define "Christian." One of my old seminary professors in Edinburgh offered this as the best test of Christian identity: "Can you agree with the statement, 'Jesus Christ is Lord'?" But others have their own tests that include belief in the authority of Christian tradition and scriptures. For example, near the end of his life, the legendary Protestant theologian Karl Barth was asked to sum up his own faith, and he quoted a Sunday School song: "Jesus loves me, this I know, for the Bible tells me so." My friends in Cape Town have taught me that people who live out the radical demands of the Christian Gospel cannot help but act as servant-leaders. They listen more than they talk, use persuasion rather than coercion and manipulation, build community, access *entheos,* work to make others healthier, freer, wiser, more autonomous and more likely themselves to become servants. By contrast, a "Sunday Christian" who separates religion from life and everyday behaviors is not necessarily a servant-leader.

Q: Does a perfect servant-leader exist anywhere?

A: No. There is no such thing as a "perfect" servant-leader, just as there is no such thing as a "perfect" Christian. Robert Greenleaf certainly never claimed to be a perfect servant-leader. Servant leadership is a practical philosophy, a journey, a worthy ideal, what one consultant called "The DNA of all approaches to ethical leadership." It is not a checklist for perfection.

Postlude

After completing this chapter, I sent it to Marlon Fortuin. His emailed response was no surprise:

> Only now do I understand why God led me one Sunday to minister a sermon titled "You Are Not Insignificant!" We are doing what we do here not for any other reason than that there's a need for it. We many times miss what a big deal it is to the person who receives, or how God answers our prayers.

A prayer answered by God is ordinary, like it is supposed to happen. We miss the miracle in it. (I'm not saying that we miss God's hand in it, but miss what we have received, and how big it is to others.)

You talk about servant leadership. Is there any other kind?

IMPLEMENTING SERVANT
LEADERSHIP:
HOW IT'S DONE

IF YOU FEEL A DEEP RESONANCE when you hear about servant leadership, a small, electric shock of recognition, you are not alone. I remember telling a classmate about servant leadership at a high school reunion, someone I always thought was a natural servant-leader. Her face lit up and she said, "This is what I've always believed! Can you imagine what a difference it would make if people operated this way at work?"

Dr. Patch Adams had the same response. At a time when the medical community thought he was nuts with his ideas on humor and health, he picked up Robert Greenleaf's essay *The Servant as Leader* and suddenly recognized that this language described who he was, deep down. Scores of other people have reported the same experience, usually followed by the question, "But is it really possible to operate with these values, especially in business?"

The good news is, it is possible. We can not only imagine the benefits of leading by serving—and choosing to follow servants—we can report them, as so many have done in these pages. "But where do I start?" ask many people. "Where is the program, the curriculum to implement servant leadership at all levels of my organization? Give me the bullet points!"

Start with the Self

Kathleen Fasbender, Jenny King, Gary Looper and TDIndustries Partners would tell you that servant leadership is not a program; it is a soulful journey. Soulfulness always starts with the self. Only then does one move out to influence the sphere that one already occupies. Kathleen Fasbender started with her personal studies before carefully designing a servant-leadership development program. Pastor Jerome Pienaar and his wife Charlene started with a commitment to their own spiritual lives and then to the people in their fractured neighborhood. Servant-leaders take radical responsibility for their personal servant behaviors first, no matter the prevailing culture, and realize that *we cannot lead people to places where we have never been.* This is in stark contrast to a comment I have heard many times in servant-leadership workshops: "This sounds great, and I certainly believe it, *but you should meet my boss!* How can I get my boss to take this seriously?" Robert Greenleaf had the answer: "If a flaw in the world is to be remedied, to the servant the process of change starts in *here,* in the servant, not *out there.*"[1]

But then what? How can we begin to introduce servant leadership to an organization with the goal that these values are not only reflected in individuals but in system-wide policies, the way they are at TDIndustries? The following guidelines are gleaned from years of conversations with people who are on the front lines of implementing servant leadership.

Live It First

Gandhi said it best: "Be the change you seek to create." This is how we *learn and earn.*

We *learn* to break the reactive, "on automatic" responses to stressful situations. You know the drill. A spouse or co-worker says something that seems unfair or just plain wrong. Something churns in the gut. You want to jump in and correct them, defend yourself, say, "Do it my way or hit the highway!" There may be a place for this response in a true emergency situation, but other than that, it almost never builds people, makes them "healthier, wiser, freer, more autonomous, and more likely themselves to become servants," to quote Greenleaf's best test for a servant-leader. By contrast, Greenleaf says, "A natural servant-leader always responds to a problem by listening *first.*"[2]

By being the change we seek to create, we also *earn* moral authority. Moral authority is the legitimate power bestowed upon us by others because of who we are and what we consistently do. Aristotle called moral authority (character or *ethos*) a more powerful tool for persuasion than emotional appeals (*pathos*) or logical arguments (*logos*).

Learning to change our responses and *earning* trust from others requires maturity, the maturity of an evolving self that has shifted from a focus on ego to a focus on the needs of others and the greater good. Or, as my friends Donna and Jerry Govan put it, "Take the 'E' out of Ego and GO!" One cannot simply tell others about maturity-beyond-ego, but must demonstrate it.

During the first residency of the Ken Blanchard Executive MBA Program housed at Grand Canyon University in Phoenix, Dr. Blanchard personally leads an exercise he calls "Egomaniacs Anonymous."[3] Ken, who has over forty million books in print, is the first to stand and say, "Hi! I'm Ken, and I'm an egomaniac!" Such admissions are how we earn moral authority and break the chains of old, destructive, automatic responses. Learners who enter Viterbo University's Master of Arts in Servant Leadership Program participate in similar experiences—deep sharing of personal glories and shadows and reflections, all the while making connections between academic learning, personal growth and real-life applications.

Find Allies for Study, Reflection and Practice

The basics of servant leadership are deceptively simple: a servant-leader serves first and then chooses to lead as a way of serving. But this way of leading, living and loving has wide-ranging ramifications in one's personal life, in relationships and policies in the workplace, and in the wider community. Servant leadership is not a fad or the latest "change initiative" mandated from the top down, not if it works. I have never seen it implemented in an organization without one or more small groups first spending significant time reading, reflecting and sharing possibilities for its practice and implementation.

But we live in the real world. What if top management does not understand servant leadership and shows no interest? A servant-leader knows that people are where they are. Perhaps some do not yet have enough information, or wonder if this servant leadership idea might threaten their power. Those people—top managers or not—deserve to be listened to. But all that any of us can control is our own sphere. One member of a servant leadership study group who initially faced questions from his boss told me, "We just decided to start where we were, with whoever shared our interest in servant leadership. That's all we could control, and is all that any of us can control. We kept top management informed on a regular basis and eventually were invited to make a presentation to the organization's leadership team about what we were learning."

It is fair to say, however, that serious implementation of servant leadership in an organization, or even in a development class like Kathy Fasbender created, eventually requires support from those who must approve such things. The best strategy is to get permission to begin and keep them informed along the way.

When I first began working in servant leadership, reading materials were limited to Greenleaf's writings and a few stray magazine articles. Today, there are enough publications on the topic to make a seeker wonder where to start. Many groups begin with Greenleaf's original essay, *The Servant as Leader*. Although Greenleaf writes clearly, this is not a quick read; it is to be savored, not skimmed. In the latest edition, the Greenleaf Center for Servant Leadership offers discussion questions that will begin the process of asking questions. *The Servant as Leader* and several other helpful writings are referenced in the notes for this chapter.[4]

Here is one of the best tips I have ever heard from a small group: Each member makes a commitment to implement at least one principle of servant leadership immediately, *that day,* and then shares the experience with group members at the next meeting. Since Greenleaf said listening was the premier skill of a servant-leader, that is a good first assignment. Be sure you understand what Greenleaf means by "listening" (details in chapter six), because he goes beyond the tips and techniques of "active listening."

Be Patient

Servant leadership is not a project to implement, but a journey to be started. It takes time.

I worked with one state-wide health care system that included sixty-eight organizations, from major hospitals to nursing homes to small clinics, and they invested two years in discussing servant leadership before implementing their own version of it. Why so long? "We needed consensus from every organization in our system before we implemented a new vision and mission and began to change operating policies that embodied those values," the CEO told me. She and her team knew better than to seek "buy-in" after the fact from employees who had had no hand in fashioning the new orientation to servant leadership. Not every employee agreed with every change, but at least they had their say, and felt heard.

Do Your Own Thing

Every organization implements servant leadership differently, and that is a good thing, because every one of them has a different history, culture and ethos.

Some organizations, like a Fortune 500 company with which I worked, can look to the profound humanity and natural servanthood of a founder and draw inspiration from that person's ethical—and profitable—behavior.

Others need a wake-up call to begin thinking about leadership in a different way, like the trucking company that still operated under the old power-based model begun by its founder, whom I'll call Elmer. Elmer was a good person, but he grew up in an era when a boss's main role was understood to be a taskmaster who made lazy employees toe the line. Problem was, after unpleasant encounters with management, company drivers felt so discounted, frustrated, angry and preoccupied that they had a series of small accidents, so many, in fact, that the company's insurer cancelled coverage. No insurance, no trucking company. Simple as that. The owner blamed the drivers; they blamed him.

Meanwhile, everyone had to change—*really* change—their attitudes, or they would all be out of a job. With some outside consultation, the company was able to self-insure while diving into the hard work of listening to and respecting each other. Knowing that there was no quick fix to the situation, the consultants helped the company create internal systems that supported long-term transformation. Eventually the founder saw positive results and decided that there may be something worthwhile in this servant leadership stuff. No one could have forced him to change his attitude about this. He had to make that internal movement on his own.

After reading *The Servant as Leader,* one founder/CEO told me his company realized they needed to "operationalize Greenleaf" because he did not provide all the answers. It was up to them to decide what difference these ideas would make. He and his people also read Covey, Senge and many other authors, and made the connections to servant leadership and to their own engineering business. That is the way to do it.

Biggest Mistakes

After learning how others have successfully implemented servant leadership, some common mistakes are obvious. *Impatience* heads the list.

The leadership team of one hospital took a vote and decided that their organization was going follow the principles of servant leadership from now on, and immediately sent out a press release announcing that fact before they shared it with employees! When employees read it in the paper, they were naturally suspicious because of their experience with some of the leadership team members, and the project died on the vine. By trying to be revolutionary rather than evolutionary, the management team lost its moral authority.

A related mistake is sometimes made by people who *can violate the principles of servant leadership in the process of implementing servant leadership!* Good intentions do not inoculate us from the temptation to use that old coercive power model of leadership. We want to *make* others see that this is a good thing, *see* that it is the *right* thing, *push* for acceptance. When that happens, take a deep breath. Smile at yourself, then begin the thoughtful, reflective process of using what Dr. Kent Keith, CEO of the Greenleaf Center in Indianapolis, calls the "service model of leadership," because if you do not, all is lost. No one will believe what you say, just what you do.

I have also seen people who catch fire with servant leadership develop what I would call *creeping grandiosity*. "I (or we) have The Answer! If you don't agree, you are not part of the in group." The unbridled enthusiasm of a recent convert can be destructive to both one's moral authority and the positive transformation of one's institution. No one has all the answers, including Robert Greenleaf—or as he would say, *especially* Robert Greenleaf!

Finally, because servant leadership is a serious topic, many people *do not keep it fun.* Greenleaf, quoting one of his former bosses at AT&T, said this about work: "If it ain't fun, it won't get done!" Even though Greenleaf himself was a serious person, he had a knack for claiming celebration and playfulness in the middle of it all. Southwest Airlines does the same thing. Southwest is arguably America's most financially successful airline, yet their employees make time for fun and celebration on a regular basis. Even the PA announcements on Southwest flights mix humor and serious instructions.

Expand on the Basic Recipe

Great chefs learn basic recipes and then expand upon them by infusing them with their own experience, style and taste. That is the same process we've seen with people in organizations that implement servant leadership; first learn the basics, then modify, experiment, get feedback and finally serve the dish, knowing that it can always be improved in the future.

So here is the basic recipe for implementing servant leadership: learn it, live it, share it, modify it for your own organization, be patient with it—and yourself—and do not forget to have fun. The rest is up to you.

❧ 6 ❧

SERVANT LEADERSHIP:
AN EXECUTIVE PRIMER

EOPLE WHO FIRST HEAR THE PHRASE *servant-leader*
naturally ask, "What does it mean, especially for businesses?" Fair enough, but be warned that it is a catchy term
with big arms that can embrace multiple meanings. Dozens of writers have tried their hand at decoding Greenleaf.
Nearly all of their bullet-point lists are right, as far as they
go, but none are complete. Perhaps this is as it should be,
because Greenleaf was not a bullet-point kind of thinker,
and perhaps no such list could be complete. Still, servant
leadership is based on universal principles that apply to
individuals, businesses and organizations of all kinds, including religious groups. The short primer that follows
uses Greenleaf's own words as much as possible.

Who and What Is a Leader?

For openers, begin with a leader—any leader. Greenleaf
says a leader is one who "goes out ahead and shows the
way...He says, 'I will go, follow me!' when he knows that

the path is uncertain, even dangerous."[1] The leader is open to inspiration, but "the leader needs more than inspiration...He initiates, provides the ideas and the structure, and takes the risk of failure along with the chance of success."[2]

The leader always knows the goal and "can articulate it for any who are unsure. By clearly stating and restating the goal the leader gives certainty and purpose to others who may have difficulty in achieving it for themselves... The word *goal* is used here in the special sense of the overarching purpose, the big dream, the visionary concept, the ultimate consummation which one approaches but never really achieves."[3]

People follow leaders because they believe leaders "see more clearly where it is best to go."[4] In that sense, followers make the leaders. Hitler was a leader, but his vision of where to go was ethically warped. Still, he could not have accomplished what he did without followers who not only believed in his goal, but coerced unbelievers into followership.

How does one "see more clearly where it is best to go"? Through *foresight*. "Foresight is the 'lead' that the leader has. Once he loses this lead and events start to force his hand, he is leader in name only. He is not leading; he is reacting to immediate events and he probably will not long be a leader."[5] Machiavelli knew this. Here is his advice to princes who wished to survive, quoted by Greenleaf in a modern paraphrase: "Thus it happens in matters of state; for knowing afar off (which it is only given a prudent man to do) the evils that are brewing, they are easily cured. But when, for want of such knowledge, they are allowed to grow so that everyone can recognize them, there is no longer any remedy to be found."[6]

By this definition a leader can be moral or amoral, kind or cruel. Mother Teresa, Winston Churchill and Ivan the Terrible were all leaders. In defining servant leadership, Greenleaf takes the common notion of heroic leadership (known in leadership circles as "The Great Man" theory) and turns it on its head.

Who Is a Servant-Leader?

Greenleaf's first servant writing was titled "The Servant as Leader," not "The Leader as Servant." Greenleaf explains the difference:

> The servant-leader is servant first...It begins with the natural feeling that one wants to serve, to serve *first*. Then conscious choice brings one to aspire to lead. That person is sharply different from one who is leader first, perhaps because of the need to assuage an unusual power drive or to acquire material possessions. For such it will be a later choice to serve—after leadership is established. The leader-first and the servant-first are two extreme types. Between them there are shadings and blends that are part of the infinite variety of human nature...The difference manifests itself in the care taken by the servant-first to make sure that other people's highest priority needs are being served.[7]

Even though motives are critical to one's identity as a servant-leader, personal qualities are not enough. The "best test" of a servant-leader is one of sheer pragmatism, based on mostly-observable outcomes.

> The best test, and difficult to administer, is: do those served grow as persons; do they, while being served, become healthier, wiser, freer, more autonomous, more likely themselves to become servants? And, what is the effect on the least privileged in society; will he benefit, or, at least, will he not be further deprived?[8]

Neither Greenleaf's definition of a servant-leader nor its best test requires one to hold a formal leadership position. What matters is what we do in "our little corner of the world"—as Greenleaf often said—and why we are doing it. In his workshops, Richard Smith, a former colleague at the Greenleaf Center and a thoughtful Greenleaf scholar, teaches that servant leadership "turns leadership into a territory," a field of action in which various people can operate depending upon their individual abilities and capacities to serve the mission of the enterprise and the people who make it all happen.

Competencies of the Servant-Leader

Few of the competencies of a servant-leader are taught in schools. If they are, they are often reduced to formulas.

Listening is the premier skill, even though Greenleaf sees it as more than a skill. "Listening might be defined as an attitude toward other people and what they are attempting to express."[9] "I have a bias about this," he writes, "which suggests that only a true natural servant automatically responds to any problem by listening first. When he is a leader, this disposition causes him to be seen as servant first. This suggests that a non-servant who wants to be a servant might become a natural servant through a long arduous discipline of learning to listen, a discipline sufficiently sustained that the automatic response to any problem is to listen first."[10] Greenleaf does not want his notion of listening to be confused with mere tips and techniques: "Listening isn't just keeping quiet; and it isn't just making appropriate responses that indicate one is awake and paying attention. Listening is a healing attitude, the attitude of intensely holding the belief—faith if you wish to call it thus—that the person or persons being listened to will rise to the challenge of grappling with the issues involved in finding their own wholeness."[11]

Servant-leaders use power ethically, with persuasion as the preferred mode. Persuasion "involves arriving at a feeling of rightness about a belief or action through one's own intuitive sense...The act of persuasion, thus defined, would help order the logic and favor the intuitive step. But *the person being persuaded* must take that intuitive step alone, untrammeled by coercive or manipulative stratagems of any kind."[12]

Greenleaf recognized that there were times when manipulation, and perhaps even coercion, were in order, but only when it involved the well-being of others or institutional survival, not for the purpose of inflating one's ego. Persuasion is not easy. It is, "on a critical issue, a difficult, time-consuming process. It demands one of the most exacting of human skills."[13]

When possible, a servant-leader seeks consensus in group decisions. "Consensus is used in its commonly understood meaning of unanimity or general agreement in matters of opinion, as opposed to taking a vote," says Greenleaf. "Individuals either accept the decision as the right or best one, or they agree to support it as a feasible resolution of the issue…the individual's position is intuitively derived in the absence of any coercive pressure to conform."

To further consensus, a servant-leader must be able to: (1) deeply understand the issue under consideration and articulate it clearly and succinctly, (2) listen, (3) "decide when it is feasible to begin to search for consensus. This may be early or late in the discussion," and (4) decide when it is feasible to adjourn to speak privately with remaining holdouts, realizing that holdouts "may be of great value, but they may function best as lone workers or in groups that operate by majority rule."[14]

A servant leader practices foresight. We have already seen that foresight is a core skill for all leaders. For servant-leaders, Greenleaf believes that foresight is the central ethic of leadership.

> The failure (or refusal) of a leader to foresee may be viewed as an ethical failure; because a serious ethical compromise today (when the usual judgment on ethical inadequacy is made) is sometimes the result of a failure to make the effort at an earlier date to foresee today's events and take the right actions when there was freedom for initiative to act… By this standard a lot of guilty people are walking around with an air of innocence that they would

not have if society were able always to pin the label "unethical" on the failure to foresee and the consequent failure to act constructively when there was freedom to act.[15]

One need not look far to see how short-term thinking and lack of foresight have led to business failures, bankrupt government policies and individual ruin. In fact, Greenleaf believed prudent foresight could have gone a long way toward saving AT&T from its break-up.

Greenleaf's view of foresight was somewhat nontraditional. Imagine time as a line drawn from the dim past to the infinite future. Now is but one point on the line, a point which moves incessantly towards the future like a tireless rabbit chasing a carrot just out of reach. Here is the nontraditional part—imagine a flashlight beam focused on now, moving with the action. The beam is most intense at the present moment, but it also illuminates part of the past and the future. "'Now' includes all of this," says Greenleaf, "all of history and all of the future. As I view it, it simply gradually intensifies in the degree of illumination as this moment of clock time is approached."[16] Knowing history helps us understand patterns of the past. Foresight, based on intuition, can help us tentatively understand and predict patterns of the future. Paradoxically, one must live fully in the now, with high awareness of conscious and non-conscious realities and potentials, to access information about the future. Given these conditions, everyone can learn the art of foresight.

A servant-leader uses language in a way that avoids the "closed verbal worlds" of narrow disciplines or cults. Specifically, she "must have facility in tempting the hearer into that leap of imagination that connects the verbal concept to the hearer's own experience. The limitation on language, to the communicator, is that the hearer must make that leap of imagination…Many attempts to communicate are nullified by saying too much."[17]

Servant-leaders practice the art of withdrawal. Withdrawal serves leaders who love intense pressure as well as those who do not. We can assume the intention for both kinds of leaders is to perform at one's optimum, a state that Greenleaf defines as "that pace and set of choices that give one the best performance over a lifespan." To reach optimum performance "out there" in the world, a servant-leader, paradoxically, goes "in here," seeking the quiet which allows deep wisdom and intuition to emerge.

"That sounds great, but you should see my schedule!" many will object. Greenleaf suggests another skill to enable withdrawal. "The ability to withdraw and reorient oneself, if only for a moment, presumes that one has learned the art of *systematic neglect*, to sort out the more important from the less important—and the important from the urgent—and attend to the more important."[18]

A servant-leader practices acceptance and empathy, even with difficult people. To a large extent, a servant-leader's greatness and effectiveness relies upon her ability to accept and empathize, which, as Greenleaf explains, does not mean she always accepts behaviors.

> The servant as leader always empathizes, always accepts the person but sometimes refuses to accept some of the person's effort or performance as good enough.[19]

It is part of the enigma of human nature that the "typical" person—immature, stumbling, inept, lazy—is capable of great dedication and heroism *if* he is wisely led. Many otherwise able people are disqualified to lead because they cannot work with and through the half-people, who are all there are. The secret of institution building is to be able to weld a team of such people by lifting them up to grow taller than they would otherwise be.[20]

Conceptualizing is an ability that requires more than verbal skills. Greenleaf called it the prime leadership talent. The conceptualizer has "the ability to see the whole in the perspective of history—past and future—to state and adjust goals, to evaluate, to analyze, and to foresee contingencies a long way ahead…The conceptualizer, at his or her best, is a persuader and a relation builder."[21]

By contrast, much of management is accomplished through the skills of "operators," who have "the ability to carry the enterprise toward its objectives in the situation, from day to day, and resolve the issues that arise as this movement takes place." Organizations need the skills of both operators and conceptualizers. The latter are often passed over for promotion in this can-do world, but they "usually emerge when an organization makes a strong push for distinction."[22]

Servant-leaders nurture community. "Living in community as one's basic involvement will generate an exportable surplus of love which the individual may carry into his many involvements with institutions which are usually not communities: businesses, churches, governments, schools."[23] Community is diminished when its members limit their liability for each other. It is enhanced when "the liability of each for the other and all for one is unlimited, or as close to it as it is possible to get."[24]

"Unlimited liability." Strange words in a society where individuals and institutions seek to limit liability, words judged as unwise to many a lawyer's ear. Still, it is a requirement of love, which is something we say we want more of in private and public life. "As soon as one's liability for another is qualified *to any degree,* love is diminished by that much."[25]

A servant-leader chooses to lead. The enemy is "not evil people. Not stupid people. Not apathetic people. Not the 'system.' Not the protesters, the disrupters, the revolutionaries, the reactionaries...*In short, the enemy is strong natural servants who have the potential to lead but do not lead, or who choose to follow a non-servant.*"[26] Followers will appear—will, in fact, make the leader—"because [servant-leaders] are proven and trusted as servants."[27]

Servant Leadership in the World

In his 1972 essay *The Institution as Servant,* which was directed to businesses, universities and churches, Greenleaf expands the idea of an individual servant-leader by suggesting that institutions should also function as servants.

> This is my thesis: caring for persons, the more able and the less able serving each other, is the rock upon which a good society is built. Whereas, until recently, caring was largely person to person, now most of it is mediated through institutions—often large,

complex, powerful, impersonal; not always competent; sometimes corrupt. If a better society is to be built, one that is more just and more loving, one that provides greater creative opportunity for its people, then the most open course is to *raise both the capacity to serve and the very performance as servant* of existing major institutions by new regenerative forces operating within them.[28]

One might ask how such a thing is possible, or if it is even desirable. Greenleaf makes the case that "with the present level of education, and the extent of information sources, too many people judge our institutions as not meeting the standard of what is reasonable and possible in their service."[29] He points his finger at three culprits: trustees who don't care enough for their institutions and the people in them, institutions organized around the idea of a single chief, and lack of trust.

He claims that trustees—board members—are the "prime movers in institutional regeneration" when they accept full responsibility for the fate of the organization, ask the right "big picture" questions that lead to clear institutional goals and strategic plans, and employ staff answerable only to the board.[30]

In place of a single chief—a heroic figure who wields king-like power from the top of the organizational pyramid—Greenleaf suggests an organizational structure based on the ancient Roman notion of *primus inter pares,* "first among equals." Greenleaf explains: "What is proposed here for the top leadership team of large institutions is a shift from the hierarchical principle, with one chief, to a team of equals with a *primus* (a 'first'), preceded by the change in trustee attitude and the role necessary to assure its success."[31]

As for trust, board directors (trustees)—and everyone else in the organization—should hold the institution "in trust," but they must also trust each other. "This must come first," says Greenleaf. "Trust is first. Nothing will move until trust is firm."[32]

In his third essay, *Trustees as Servants* (1974), Greenleaf expands on how trustees can exercise a servant role, becoming more proactive rather than reactive, closely overseeing operational use of power without micromanaging, operating by consensus in their own proceedings, gathering their own information, employing a trustee coach and claiming their own power.

> Having power (and every trustee has some power) one *initiates* the means whereby power is used to serve and not to hurt. *Serve* is used in the sense that anyone touched by the institution or its work becomes, because of that influence, healthier, wiser, freer, more autonomous, more likely themselves to become servants…What shall one do, as a trustee who is aware of this necessity, if one finds that one cannot persuade one's fellow trustees to accept such an obligation, and if one does not foresee the possibility of doing so in a reasonable period? *My advice is to resign.*[33]

In later years, Greenleaf suggested an "Institute of Chairing" be established to prepare people to chair boards—and other groups—using the strategies of *primus inter pares* and consensus decision-making. He eventually concluded that organizations that train religious leaders could be the levers to change society if they taught the skills, capacities and strategies necessary for servant-leaders to operate in the wider world. If ritual leaders of churches, synagogues and mosques modeled and taught such ideas, and demanded distinction of their own religious institutions, the ripple effect could change our society into one which was more serving. It was an idea with which virtually no one agreed.

Bob Greenleaf had much more to say about how servant leadership could operate in business, education, foundations, churches and the society at large—those resources are annotated in the bibliography of *Robert K. Greenleaf: A Life of Servant Leadership*—but the basics are to be found in his first three essays: *The Servant as Leader, The Institution as Servant* and *Trustees as Servants.* These writings comprise the first three chapters of the Paulist Press book *Servant Leadership* (1977 and 2002).

Chapter One

1. In 1992, the Tomah VA served 8,000 military veterans. By 2005, the number had soared to 22,0000. According to *Time* magazine, the same thing happened nationally. From 1996 to 2006, the number of veterans receiving VA medical services doubled, while the number of employees serving them was reduced by 10,000. See Douglas Waller, "How Veteran's Hospitals Became the Best in Health Care," *Time,* August 27, 2006.; http://www.time.com/time/magazine/article/0,9171,1376238,00.html.

Chapter Two

1. TDIndustries website: http://www.tdindustries.com/cultures-values.aspx.

2. Ashley Cheshire, *Partnership of the Spirit: The Story of Jack Lowe and TDIndustries* (Dallas, TX: Taylor Publishing Company, 1987), 123.

3. *Ibid.*, 126–127.

4. From http://www.tdindustries.com/cultures-values.aspx:

Mission
TDIndustries customers and employees work together to fulfill our mission: We are committed to providing outstanding career opportunities by exceeding our customers' expectations through continuous aggressive improvement.

Values
Servant Leaders are active listeners...they elicit trust...and share power. Our Basic Values listed below are the most important characteristic of TDIndustries and guide all of our relationships—with our customers, our suppliers, our communities, and among ourselves.

- Concern for and Belief in Individual Human Beings
- Valuing Individual Differences
- Honesty
- Building Trusting Relationships
- Fairness
- Responsible Behavior
- High Standards of Business Ethics

And we don't stop there...We believe in:

- Long term goals—we do not seize short term benefits to the detriment of our long term mission.
- Continuous, intense people-development efforts, including substantial training budgets.
- Investment in tools, equipment and facilities that enable us to better accomplish our mission.

5. Here is the full list of TDIndustries' servant leadership principles, found at: http://www.tdindustries.com/servantleadership.aspx:

A brief account of Greenleaf's philosophy teaches us that:

- People can and should work together to grow a company. If an organization is to live up to its basic values and vision, a key ingredient will be leadership from all of us.
- Simply and plainly defined, leaders are people who have followers. They have earned recognition and respect.
- Leaders are first a servant of those they lead. They are a teacher, a source of information and knowledge, and a standard setter, more than a giver of directions or a disciplinarian.
- Leaders see things through the eyes of their followers. They put themselves in others' shoes and help them make their dreams come true.
- Leaders do not say, "Get going." Instead, they say, "Let's go!" and lead the way. They do not walk behind with a whip; they are out in front with a banner.
- Leaders assume that their followers are working with them. They consider others to be their partners in the work and see to it that they share in the rewards and they glorify the team spirit.
- Leaders are people builders. They help people to grow because the leader realizes that the

more people grow, the stronger the organization will be.

- Leaders do not hold people down… they lift them up. They reach out their hand to help their followers scale the peaks.
- Leaders have faith in people. They believe in them. They have found that others will rise to high expectations.
- Leaders use their heart as well as their head. After they have looked at the facts with their head, they let their heart take a look too.
- Leaders keep their eyes on high goals. They are self-starters. They create plans and set them in motion. They are people of thought and action—both dreamers and doers.
- Leaders are faced with many hard decisions, including balancing fairness to an individual with fairness to the group. This sometimes requires "weeding out" those in the group who, over a period of time, do not measure up to the group needs of dependability, productivity and safety.
- Leaders have a sense of humor. They are not stuffed shirts. They can laugh at themselves. They have a humble spirit.
- Leaders can be led. They are not interested in having their own way, but in finding the best way. They have an open mind.

6. For more on the work of Dr. McGee-Cooper & Associates, visit: http://www.amca.com .

7. Gary Looper, interview with the author, June 26, 2008.

8. See Stephen M. R. Covey, with Rebecca R. Merrill, *The Speed of Trust: The One Thing that Changes Everything,* (New York: Free Press, 2008).

9. Bob Ferguson, interview with the author, June 26, 2008.

10. Information on the Trust Index may be found on the website of the Great Place to Work® Institute, http://www.greatplacetowork.com/consulting/trust-index.php .

11. Cheshire, 134–35.

Chapter Three

1. Jennifer King, "Born to Be Me: My Search for Vocation," in *Becoming Authentic: The Search for Wholeness and Calling as a Servant-Leader,* ed. Trevor M. Hall (South Bend, IN: Cloverdale Books, 2007), 41.

2. Howard Behar, *It's Not About the Coffee: Leadership Principles from a Life at Starbucks* (NY: The Penguin Group, Portfolio Hardcover, 2007), 1–2.

3. "History of Coffee," Nestle, U. K. website. Accessed August 19, 2008 at http://www.nestle.co.uk/OurBrands/AboutOurBrands/Beverages/History+of+Coffee.htm .

4. "Café Frauenhuber Chronicle." Accessed August 17, 2008 at http://www.cafefrauenhuber.com/common-en/chronik.php .

5. Website of Le Procope Bistro/Restaurant/Café. Accessed August 19, 2008 at http://home.att.net/~sakal/pages/procope.htm . See also the Wikipedia article on the history of coffee at http://en.wikipedia.org/wiki/Coffeehouse.

6. "History," Lloyd's of London website. Accessed August 29, 2008 at http://www.lloyds.com/About_Us/History/Chronology.htm .

7. King, 38.

8. James Autry, *The Servant Leader: How to Build a Creative Team, Develop Great Morale, and Improve Bottom-Line Performance* (New York: Three Rivers Press, 2004).

9. King, 38.

Chapter Four

1. Bill Bottom, interview with the author, Ann Arbor, Michigan, 21 July, 1999.

2. Robert K. Greenleaf, *On Becoming a Servant Leader: The Private Writings of Robert K. Greenleaf,* ed. Don M. Frick and Larry C. Spears (San Francisco: Jossey-Bass, 1996), 344.

3. See David S. Young, *Servant Leadership for Church Renewal: Shepherds by the Living Springs* (Scottsdale, PA: Herald Press, 1999) and *Springs of Living Water: Christ-Centered Church Renewal* (Scottsdale, PA: Herald Press, 2008).

4. Marlon Fortuin, unpublished manuscript, *Move Towards God and His Purposes,* 2008.

5. After the days when Greenleaf studied and befriended both ministers, Phil Tom was tapped to head up the urban ministry efforts of the Presbyterian Church (USA) and Dr. Amerson was appointed president of Claremont Theological School in Claremont, California (2000–2006), and in 2006 was appointed president of Garrett-Evangelical Theological Seminary in Evanston, Illinois.

6. The distinction between "doing church" and "being the church" is explored in Albert L. Winesman, *Growing an Engaged Church: How to Stop Doing Church and Start Being the Church* (New York: Gallup Press, 2007).

7. Greenleaf first wrote about *entheos* in a short book he titled *The Ethic of Strength* that sat in his files for 35 years before being discovered and published in *On Becoming a Servant Leader* (pp. 13–105). He also mentions *entheos* in his essay *The Servant as Leader.* As Greenleaf studied the lives of people he considered exemplary servant-leaders, like Pope John XXIII and Nikolaj Frederik Severin (N.F.S.) Gruntvig, the activist who revolutionized Danish society in the early nineteenth century by starting "schools of spirit," he noticed that servant-leaders were sustained by an inner spirit that could—and often did—come from a religious tradition, but also seemed to transcend doctrine. He uses the word *entheos* in this most personal *and* transcendent sense.

Chapter Five

1. Robert K. Greenleaf, *The Servant as Leader* (1970; Indianapolis: The Greenleaf Center for Servant Leadership, 1991), 34.

2. See chapter six in this volume, "Servant Leadership: An Executive Primer."

3. The website for the Ken Blanchard Executive MBA program is http://emba.gcu.edu .

4. The Greenleaf Center for Servant Leadership in Indianapolis is the starting place for learning materials on servant leadership (www.greenleaf.org). Greenleaf's essay *The Servant as Leader* may be purchased separately with discussion questions included, or you can read it as the first chapter in the book Robert K. Greenleaf, *Servant Leadership: A Journey into the Nature of Legitimate Power and Greatness* (Mahwah, NJ: Paulist Press, 1977).

Chapter Six

This chapter is excerpted from Don M. Frick, *Robert K. Greenleaf: A Life of Servant Leadership* (San Francisco: Berrett-Koehler, 2004). Permission is granted to reproduce and distribute this chapter with the publication attribution intact.

1. Greenleaf, *The Servant as Leader*, 8.
2. *Ibid.*
3. *Ibid.*, 9.
4. *Ibid.*, 8.
5. *Ibid.*, 18.
6. *Ibid.*, 17.
7. *Ibid.*, 7.
8. *Ibid.*
9. Greenleaf, *On Becoming a Servant-Leader*, 70.
10. Greenleaf, *The Servant as Leader*, 10.
11. Greenleaf, *On Becoming a Servant-Leader*, 95.
12. *Ibid.*, 129 (italics added).
13. *Ibid.*, 14.
14. Greenleaf, *On Becoming a Servant-Leader*, 141–3.
15. Greenleaf, *The Servant as Leader*, 16.
16. Greenleaf, *On Becoming a Servant-Leader*, 317.
17. Greenleaf, *The Servant as Leader*, 11.
18. *Ibid.*, 12 (italics added).
19. *Ibid.*, 12–13.
20. *Ibid.*, 13–14.
21. Greenleaf, *On Becoming a Servant-Leader*, 217.
22. *Ibid.*
23. Greenleaf, *The Servant as Leader*, 29.
24. *Ibid.*
25. *Ibid.*

26. *Ibid.*, 34–5 (italics in original).

27. *Ibid.*, 4.

28. Robert K. Greenleaf, *The Institution as Servant* (1972; Indianapolis: Greenleaf Center for Servant Leadership, 1976), 1 (italics in original).

29. *Ibid.*, 6.

30. *Ibid.*, 6–8.

31. *Ibid.*, 12.

32. *Ibid.*, 34.

33. Robert K. Greenleaf, *Trustees as Servants* (1974; Indianapolis: Greenleaf Center for Servant Leadership, 1991), 37 (italics in original).

CONTACTS

You may contact Bob Ferguson of TDIndustries at bob. ferguson@tdindustries.com and servant leadership consultant Gary Looper at gary@amca.com.

Kathleen Fasbender remains active in servant leadership development activities. You can reach her at fasbender@ charter.net.

You may contact Jennifer King at jk6string@gmail.com.

For more information on the work of my business friend and his nonprofit ministry, in Cape Town, plus videos of some of the Clarke's Estate residents mentioned in the chapter, visit: www.screwupsforgod.com.

Don M. Frick's e-mail address is: don@donfrick.com.

Printed in Great Britain
by Amazon